Die Möglichkeit, mit der Kamera Ereignisse zu
dokumentieren und zu beschreiben, hat der Fotografie
schon immer eine einzigartige Macht gegenüber
anderen Kunstformen gegeben.
Das ist Wahrheit.   Martha Hill

Alle Fotografien in diesem Buch sind Original-
aufnahmen, die nicht digital verändert wurden.
                                                    Fritz Pölking

The possibility to document and describe events with
a camera has always given the art of photography
a unique power in comparison to other forms of art.
That is truth.   Martha Hill

All Photographs in this book are original takes that
have not been digitally altered.   Fritz Pölking

Internet:
www.poelking.com
www.kildaverlag.de
www.tecklenborg-verlag.de
www.mandusa.com

Impressum

In die englische Sprache übertragen
von Rosi Hoffmann
- www.mandusa.com -

Layout: Jan Tölle

© Kilda-Verlag, D-48268 Greven, Germany
- Info@kildaverlag.de -
Alle Rechte vorbehalten. 2004.
All rights reserved. 2004.

ISBN 3-88949-201-0

Printed in Germany 2004

Gesamtherstellung:
Druckhaus Tecklenborg, Steinfurt

Fritz Pölking

Am Puls des Lebens

At the Pulse of Life

Kilda-Verlag

Vorwort

„Am Puls des Lebens" zeigt Momente in der Natur, die von allen Künsten nur die Naturfotografie so festhalten kann. Nur sie kann das Spektakel der Wirklichkeit, wie etwa die Essenz von Bewegung, sichtbar machen. Das macht sie einmalig und unverwechselbar.

Die folgenden Seiten zeigen solche Augenblicke aus der Natur: spannende, schöne, humorvolle, informative oder dramatische.

Natur lebt im Augenblick. Vergangenheit betrifft sie nur, soweit sie sie geformt und verändert hat. Das Leben in der Natur ist Gegenwart, und daher wie kaum etwas anderes geeignet, um mit dem Medium Fotografie festgehalten zu werden.

Der Naturfotograf als Journalist mit der Kamera ist in der Lage dies schnell, korrekt, nuanciert und gestaltend zu tun. Wir brauchen Aufnahmen wie diese, um uns ein zutreffendes Bild vom Leben in der Wirklichkeit zu machen. Sie zeigen uns, welch ein grandioses Spektakel das Leben ist, und – daß die Dinge des Lebens sich wiederholen.

Diese Bilder zeigen den Teil im Alltag des Lebens, der keine Nachrichten produziert. Deshalb gibt es diese Fotografien aus der Natur, die uns erfreuen, erstaunen oder entsetzen, denn sie sind ein wichtiges Regulativ zu den 'manipulierten Bildern und verstümmelten Wahrheiten', mit denen wir oft bedient werden.

Die Bilder evozieren die wirkliche Welt und im Kontext mit den Texten und zusätzlichen, das Thema umkreisenden fotografischen Miniaturen zeigen sie den Pulsschlag des Lebens in seiner – faszinierenden – Mechanik, und sie bestätigen was man im Laufe der Jahre erahnt, erfühlt und entdeckt hat: Es bleibt schwierig, und – die Natur ist ein Geschenk an die Fotografie.

Malerei, Musik und Literatur können vieles besser ausdrücken als die Fotografie, aber als Schilderer des Momentes, der Gegenwart in der Natur, ist die Fotografie unschlagbar.

Herzlich Ihr

Prologue

"At the Pulse of Life" shows moments within nature that, of all forms of art, can only be captured by nature photography in this specific way.

Only nature photography can show the spectacular reality that nature holds; for example, the essence of movement. This turns it into something unique and unmistakable.

The following pages will show you just such moments out of nature: exciting, beautiful, humorous, informative and dramatic.

Nature lives for the moment. The past will only apply as far as having been formed and changed by her. Life within nature is the here and now and that is the reason why she is suited far better then hardly anything else to be captured by the medium of photography.

The nature photographer as journalist with a camera is able to do this quickly, correctly, in detail and organized.

We need photos like these in order to have a fitting picture of life within reality. They show us just what a grand spectacle life really is and – that everything in life repeats itself.

These pictures show a part of every-day-life that does not produce news coverage. That is why there are photographs of nature which please, surprise or shock us, because they are an important regulater for the "manipulated picture and mutilated truth" that we are often confronted with.

These pictures evoke the real world and in context with the writings and additional photographic miniatures that encircle the subject, show the pulse of life in its – fascinating – action, and they confirm what has been suspected, felt and discovered throughout the course of the years: it remains difficult and – just like nature herself – it is a gift to photography.

Painting, music and literature can express many things better than photography, but as a portrayer of the moment, the here and now of nature, photography is unbeatable.

Sincerely yours,

Zwischen Traum und Tag

Between dream and day

Denken ist wundervoll,
aber noch wundervoller ist das Erlebnis.
Oskar Wilde

Thinking is wonderful
but living is more wonderful
Oscar Wilde (adapted)

Die schönste Stunde des Tages ist für mich die erste am frühen Morgen. Nur schade, das man dafür zu so einer unmenschlichen Zeit aufstehen muss.

Wenn man kurz vor Sonnenaufgang durch die Heide, das Moor oder eine andere Landschaft wandert, den Fotorucksack auf dem Rücken und das Stativ in der Hand, dann möchte man mit niemanden auf der Welt tauschen. Die ersten Vögel singen zwar schon, aber der Puls des Lebens bewegt sich bei den meisten noch auf niedrigem Niveau. Die meisten Tiere sind noch nicht erwacht aus der Kälte und Dunkelheit der Nacht und vor allem in der Kleintierwelt gibt es jetzt unglaublich faszinierende Motive.

So suchte ich kurz vor Sonnenaufgang einen Graben ab nach Schmetterlingen, Libellen und Käfern, als ich diesen 'Daddy Langbein' an einem Grashalm hängen sah – über und über bedeckt mit kleinen Diamanten.

Was man meistens im Morgentau im Gras findet sind Kleinlibellen. Die großen Libellen übernachten anscheinend lieber in höheren Bäumen, und Schmetterlinge mögen auch nicht so gerne die niedrigen Regionen mit Morgentau.

Aber diese Schnake hatte einen wunderschönen Platz gefunden und sich auch so fotogen aufgehängt, das einem der Atem stockte. Bevor der Morgenwind aufkam, gelang es mir dann auch noch, dieses Traummotiv festzuhalten.

The nicest hour of the day for me is the first one, early in the morning. Too bad that you have to get up at such an ungodly hour of the day for it. When you hike through the heath, the moor or other landscapes just before sunrise, with the rucksack full of photo equipment on your back and the tripod in hand you wouldn't want to trade places with anyone in the world.

Although the first birds are already singing, the pulse of life is still at a minimum. Most animals have not yet awakened from the cold and the darkness of the night and especially the world of small animals provides you with unbelievably fascinating motifs at this time.

So I was searching a ditch for butterflies, dragonflies and bugs when I came upon this "Daddy Longlegs" hanging on a stalk of grass – completely covered with small diamonds. Small dragonflies are what you find mostly in the grass, covered with morning dew. The larger ones tend to spend the night in higher trees and butterflies do not like the lower regions with morning dew either.

But this crane fly had found a wonderful spot and placed himself in such a photogenic manner that it took your breath away. I was even able to capture this dream of a shot before the morning breeze came up.

Objectiv 3.5/180 mm, Sensia-100, Stativ-tripod, Moor, Swamp, Germany

**Natur fotografieren heißt:
Erleben aus erster Hand**

**To photograph nature means
experience at first hand**

Turn of the Millennium

Jahrtausendwende

Konfetti und Sekt waren eigentlich die Basis meiner Gedanken für den 31. Dezember 2000. Nun wollte der Lektor des Kreuz Verlages in Stuttgart gerne für ein Buch über 365 Tage Natur in dem Jahr, für den 31.12.2000 das Bild einer bestimmten Bergkiefer aus der Bastei im Nationalpark Sächsiche Schweiz bei Dresden haben.

Das passte mir nicht sonderlich, weil es erstens 720 km Fahrstrecke waren, und ich für Silvester – vorstellbar – andere Pläne hatte.

Als ich über das Motiv nachdachte, fiel mir etwas auf: Der 31.12. 2000 war nicht nur der letzte Tag des Jahres, des Jahrzehnts und des Jahrhunderts, sondern auch der letzte des Jahrtausends, und – der nächste Tag war folglich der erste Tag des neues Jahrtausends.

Warum also nicht eine Zeitbelichtung machen, sagen wir von 23.50 Uhr bis 0.10? Das würde dann ein Bild sein aus zwei Jahrtausenden! Ein frappierender Gedanke.

Einziges Problem: es wurde schon um 16.30 Uhr dunkel. Ich mußte also um spätestens 16.00 Uhr meine Kamera aufbauen und den Bildausschnitt einstellen und – anschließend fast 8 Stunden in Kälte und Dunkelheit auf einer schmalen Eisenbrücke auf Mitternacht warten...

Das Bild habe ich übrigens mit vier Blitzen aufgehellt: zwei vor Mitternacht und zwei nach Mitternacht.

Es muß schließlich alles seine Ordnung haben...

My basic thoughts on December 31st, 2000 were actually confetti and champagne. So now the editor of the Kreuz Publishing Agency in Stuttgart was asking for a picture of a certain pine tree from the Bastei at Swiss Saxony National Park, which is close to Dresden, to put into a book on 365 days of nature by December 31st, 2000.

I was not necessarily happy about that since it meant driving 720km and I did have other plans for New Years – understandably.

While I was thinking about the subject I noticed something: 12-31-2000 was not just the last day of the year or the decade or century, but also the last day of the millennium which made the next day the first one of the new millennium.

So why not a timed exposure let's say from 11.50 pm until 00.10 am? That would make it a picture of two millenniums! An astonishing thought.

Only one problem: darkness fell already at 4.30 pm. So I had to set up my camera by 4.00 pm, arrange the setting of the image and then in turn wait almost 8 hrs in the cold and dark, on a small iron bridge for midnight to come...

By the way, I used 4 flashes to brighten up the picture: two prior to midnight and two after midnight.

After all, everything should be in order...

Objectiv 3.5-4.5/24-85 mm, Blitz-flash, Sensia-100, Stativ-tripod. National Park Sächsische Schweiz, Germany

Gibt es etwas Dringlicheres als den Schutz der Natur in ihrer Rechtlosigkeit? Haben wir eine größere Aufgabe, als die Schöpfung zu bewahren und damit die Nachwelt zu schützen? Ich kenne keine.
Richard von Weizäcker

Is there anything more important then the safeguard of nature in her lack of rights? Do we have a greater task then to safe-keep creation and with that posterity? I know of nothing.
Richard von Weizäcker

That special Moment

Der besondere Moment

Wenn junge Eisvögel in ihrer Bruthöhle in der Steilwand am Bach- oder Flußufer auf die Fütterung durch die Eltern mit einem Fisch warten, dann sitzt immer ein Junges im Gang zum Kessel und wartet. Wenn es einen Fisch bekommen hat, rückt es im Uhrzeigersinn weiter, und das nächste Geschwister rückt nach.

Wenn die 6-8 Jungen dann ausfliegen, fliegen sie die ersten zwei bis drei Tagen alle zusammen hinter den Eltern her um gefüttert zu werden. Das ist ziemlich unökonomisch, weil viel geflogen werden muß, bis man an der Reihe ist und einen Fisch von Mama oder Papa erhält.

Nach drei Tagen haben dies die jungen Eisvögel kapiert und verteilen sich am Flußufer entlang und warten, das ein Altvogel kommt und sie füttert. Jetzt können sie die Energie des Fisches umsetzen in Wachstum und verbrauchen sie nicht mehr beim 'hinter den Eltern herfliegen'.

Was für den Naturfotografen bedeutet: Wenn er ein Foto machen will auf dem mehrere kleine Eisvögel zu sehen sind, dann ist dafür das Fenster nur für 2-3 Tage geöffnet.

Um diesen Zeitpunkt nicht zu verpassen, hatte ich etwa 1 km von der Brutröhre entfernt an einem Teich ein Futterbecken mit kleinen Fischen installiert, das die Eisvögel regelmäßig besuchten, und wo mir dann auch 1978 dieses Bild von drei jungen Eisvögeln gelang.

When young kingfisher wait for their parents to feed them fish in their nests on steep rocky hill sides along the banks of brooks and rivers, one of the young always sits in the corridor leading into the "bowl" and waits. Then, when it has received its fish, it moves on in a clockwise fashion and the next sibling moves into place in order to wait for the next fish. This way everyone gets their share.

When the 6-8 youngsters leave the nest to fly, they follow their parents for the first two or three days in order to get fed. That is very uneconomic because a lot of flying has to be done until it is your turn to get a fish from mom or dad. After three days the young kingfisher have realized this and spread out along the riverbanks and wait for their elders to come and feed them. Now the energy from the fish can be turned into growth and is not lost in the effort of following mom and dad.

This is what that means for the nature photographer: if he wants to take a picture with several young kingfisher then the window of opportunity is only there for those 2-3 days. In order not to miss this point in time I installed a feeding bin in a nearby pond that was visited regularly by the kingfisher about 1 km away from the nest, and filled it with small fish. That is the place where I was able to take this picture in 1978 showing three young kingfisher.

▲ *Objectiv 5,5/240 mm, Blitz – Flash 1/8000 sec. Ektachrome High Speed(23 ISO). Tarnzelt – hide / Stativ – tripod.*
▶ *Objectiv 2.8/135 mm (Ektachrome High Speed (23 ISO),Tarnzelt, hide / Stativ – tripod. Münsterland, Germany*

Pilze

**Ein Naturfotograf ist jemand
der unglücklich ist, wenn er nicht in die Natur
hinausgehen kann um zu fotografieren.**

**A nature photographer is someone who is unhappy
if he can't go into nature in order to take pictures.**

Pflanzen sind es nicht und Tiere auch nicht, aber interessant und – schwierig zu fotografieren. Als Naturfotograf liebe ich die Pilze: Sie laufen nicht davon, sie wackeln nicht im Wind, sie wachsen meisten an leicht erreichbaren Stellen, und man kann sich alle Zeit der Welt lassen, wenn man versucht, sie adäquat abzulichten.

In der Regel regnet es ja, wenn man für ein Motiv die Sonne braucht, die Sonne scheint wenn man weiches Licht benötigt, es herrscht Wind wenn man Libellen fotografieren will usw. usw. Wenn man Pilze fotografiert gibt es alle diese Probleme nicht. Licht kann man sich selber machen mit Aufhellschirm oder Elektronenblitz, und wenn die Sonne scheint gibt es Softschirme. Die Pilzfotografie ist eines der wenigen Gebiete in der Naturfotografie, wo man – fast – alles unter Kontrolle hat. Daher gibt es auch so wenig echte Naturaufnahmen von Pilzen: die Verlockunge ist sehr groß, dass Naturmotiv Pilz – was man ja eigentlich fotografieren will – zu verbessern, weil die Natur ja doch irgendwie etwas schlampig arbeitet: Also Äste entfernen, den Hintergrund säubern, die Moospolster verbessern, Details umpflanzen usw. Zum Schluß ist es dann ein 'Kunstfoto unter zuhilfenahme von natürlichen Produkten', aber leider kein Naturfoto mehr. Kismet… Nebenstehend ein echtes, unverbessertes Naturfoto.

Plants they are not, nor animals, but interesting and difficult – good to photograph. As a nature photographer I love mushrooms: they don't run off, they don't wobble in the wind, they grow mostly in easily accessible places, and one can take all the time in the world, when one tries to take adequate pictures of them.

Normally it does rain when you need the sun for a motif, the sun shines when one needs a soft light; wind prevails if one wants to photograph dragonflies, etc., etc... When one photographs mushrooms, none of these problems exist. You can make your own light with reflecting screens or an electronic flash and when the sun shines, there are softening screens. Mushroom photography is one of the few areas in nature-photography, where one has (almost) everything under control. That's why there aren't many really natural pictures of mushrooms: the temptation is great to take the natural motif mushroom – that you actually want to photograph – and improve it, because nature in some way, works a bit sloppily; therefore, remove branches, clean up the background, arrange the clumps of moss, transplant details, etc... In the end, the result is an "artificial photo with the help of natural products", but unfortunately not nature photography anymore. Kismet… Opposite, a real unimproved photo of nature.

*Beringter Buchenschleimrübling, Porcelain Mushroom, Oudemansiella mucida, Objectiv 2.8/100 mm, Velvia-50, Stativ – tripod.
National Park Bayerischer Wald, Germany*

König der Arktis

King of the Arctic

Die etwa 2.000 Eisbären von Spitz-bergen können 50-80 km in 24 Stunden wandern, und nutzen ein Gebiet von über 1.000 km in der Diagonalen im Laufe eines Jahres.
Sie fürchten sich manchmal überhaupt nicht vor Menschen, und auf Spitzbergen darf man nicht ohne Gewehr wandern, was aber nicht unbedingt Sicherheit verspricht. Denn gegen einen plötzlich auf einen einzelnen oder auf eine Gruppe Menschen los rennenden Eisbären richtet auch ein Gewehr nicht viel aus.
Daher gibt es auf Spitzbergen drei gute Ratschläge:
1. Wenn ein Eisbär kommt, veranlasse einen Bekannten davonzulaufen, dann wird der Eisbär ihn verfolgen und nicht dich.
2. Eisbären essen immer erst die Köpfe der Menschen, daher wird es nicht lange weh tun.
3. Wenn sie mit einem Freund alleine wandern, dann ziehen sie gute, schnelle Turnschuhe an. Sie werden dadurch nicht schneller sein als der Eisbär, aber vielleicht schneller als ihr Freund…
Richtig belichtete Eisbärenfotos macht man übrigens, in dem man entweder auf den Eisbären mißt und eine Blende öffnet, oder auf den ihn umgebenden Schnee, und dann 1.5 bis 2 Blenden öffnet – und dann natürlich zur Belichtung das manuelle Belichtungsprogramm nimmt, und nicht eine Belichtungsautomatik, die auch reagiert, wenn sie nicht soll.

The polar bears of Spitzbergen, about 2.000 in number, can travel up to 50-80 km in 24 hours and cross an area of over 1.000 km diagonally during the course of their life. At times they are totally fearless of humans, so on Spitzbergen you can't go anywhere without a rifle, which does not necessarily assure your safety. A rifle is not especially effective against a polar bear that suddenly charges at a person or group. That is why there are three good pieces of advice on Spitzbergen:
1. If a polar bear comes toward you, get an acquaintance to start running. The polar bear will go after him not after you.
2. Polar bears always eat the heads of humans first, so it won't hurt for very long.
3. If you are afoot with a friend on your own, be sure to use good and fast footwear. You won't be any faster then the polar bear, but maybe you can be faster then your friend…
By the way, the correct exposure for pictures of polar bears would be to measure the polar bear and open an additional aperture or you measure the surrounding snow and open an additional 1.5 to 2 apertures – then of course you use the manual exposure settings – not the automatic which reacts even when it shouldn't.

Objectiv 4.0/500 mm, Fujichrome Sensia-100, Stativ – tripod. Spitzbergen-Svalbard, Norway

Es geht rund...

It comes around...

Nicht der Bach fließt, sondern das Wasser.
Nicht die Zeit vergeht, sondern wir.
Grafitti

It is not the brook that flows, but the water.
It is not time that passes, it is us.
Graffiti

Malerei kann Kunst sein, Musik kann Kunst sein, Literatur kann Kunst sein, Fotografie kann Kunst sein – muß es aber nicht. Nicht jeder Schnappschuß ist Kunst, nicht jeder Drei-minutensong und nicht jede in Öl gemalte Zigeunerin.
Was die Fotografie allen anderen Kunstformen voraus hat ist ihre Fähigkeit, den schnell vergehenden Augenblick fest-zuhalten, Ereignisse zu dokumentieren und zu beschreiben, fotojournalistisch abzubilden und gleichzeitig dabei eine Wirklichkeit sichtbar zu machen, die ohne die Fotografie nicht existieren würde. Als Naturdokument ist – oder kann sie – einmalig sein als Kunstform. Nur sie kann diesen flüch-tigen Moment des Lebens in der Natur festhalten.
Die Naturfotografie ist ein eigenständiges Medium und eine eigenständige Kunstform. Nichts kann sich mit ihr verglei-chen und nichts kommt ihr auch nur nahe oder kann sie ersetzen – wenn sie ehrlich ist und bei sich selber bleibt. Wenn sie manipuliert, arrangiert oder digital verändert, wird sie austausch-bar und belanglos, denn verändern und ar-rangieren kann und tut jeder Maler. Darum sind auch un-sere Bücher und Zeitschriften voll von Fotos und nicht von gemalten Bildern, weil die Menschen den echten, glaub-würdigen Augenblick sehen wollen. Den wirklichen Moment festhalten zu können, daraus rührt die ungeheure Über-zeugungskraft der Naturfotografie.

Painting can be considered art, music and literature can be considered art, photography can be considered art – but not necessarily. Not every snapshot is art, not every three-minute ditty and not every gypsy girl painted in oil.
The advantage that photography has over other forms of art is the ability to capture fleeting moments, document, de-scribe and depict photo-journalistic events and at the same time visualize a reality which would not exist without pho-tography. As a document of nature it is – or can be – unique as a form of art. Only it can capture this fleeting moment of life in nature. Nature photography is an autonomous medium and an independent form of art. Nothing is com-parable to it and nothing even gets close or can replace it – if it is honest and remains true to itself.
If it gets manipulated, arranged or digitally altered, it be-comes replaceable and irrelevant because every painter can and does change and rearrange.
That is the reason why our books and magazines are full of photos and not painted pictures – because people do want to see the real and believable moment. To capture the real moment is the enormous power of conviction held by and found in nature photography.

Zeitbelichtung – time exposure, Objectiv 3.5-4.5/24-85 mm, Velvia-50, Stativ-tripod, National Park Bayerischer Wald, Germany

Dew at dawn

Morgentau

Magisch ist für mich die Stunde zwischen Traum und Tag. Wenn man sich durch das Moor bewegt, erste Vogelstimmen hörbar werden, in der absoluten Windstille alles regungslos verharrt, aber der kommende Tag schon ahnbar ist.

Weniger magisch ist für mich, das ich dafür schon um 4.00 Uhr aufstehen muss, um gegen 5.30 im Moor zu sein. Denn etwa um 6.00 Uhr wird es hell, die Sonne erscheint, die Luft erwärmt sich, und ein leichter Wind setzt dadurch ein.

Dann ist es meistens schon zu spät für Aufnahmen von Schwarzen Heidelibellen, denn dieser leichte Luftzug durch die sich erwärmende Luft genügt völlig, um alle Bilder unscharf zu machen. Denn bei der morgendlichen Libellenfotografie kommt man leicht auf Belichtungszeiten von Sekunden.

Libellen haben die unerfreuliche Angewohnheit, – fast – immer zwei Flügel flach zu legen und zwei hochzustellen. Diese hochgestellten werden dann natürlich völlig unscharf abgebildet, was auf den Fotos ziemlich scheußlich aussieht. Daher besteht die Hauptaufgabe des Fotografen darin, in der kurzen Zeit zwischen völliger Dunkelheit und brauchbarem Fotolicht – und bevor der Wind kommt – die eine unter 50 Libellen zu finden, die alle vier Flügel waagerecht hält, und auch fotografierbar – das heißt im Moor erreichbar – ist.

The hour between dream and day is magical for me. When you move through the moor, hear the first birds calling, everything is frozen in the stillness and not a breeze is moving but you can sense the approaching day.

What is not so magical for me though is that I have to get up at 4 am in order to be in the moor by 5.30 am, because at 6 am the light comes in, the sun appears and the air gets warmer, which causes a slight breeze to set in.

By then it is too late most of the time to take pictures of the black dragonflies. The slight breeze that occurs when the air gets warmer is already enough to blur any photo. It is so easy to reach exposure times measured in seconds during dragonfly photography in the early morning hours.

Dragonflies have this annoying habit to – almost – always flatten two wings and hold the other two upright. So the two wings that are upright naturally will turn out fuzzy which looks pretty awful on the photos. That is why the main job of the photographer is to take that short time span between utter darkness and usable photo light – and before the breeze sets in – to take a picture of one of about 50 dragonflies that just happens to be holding all four wings in an upright position and is available to be photographed – that means reachable, in the moor.

Objectiv 3.5-4.5/24-85 mm, Sensia-100, Stativ-tripod, Moor-swamp, Germany

Naturfotografie ist kein Roulettespiel,
mit dem man den Moment der Momente einfängt.
Je mehr man plant, je akkurater man arbeitet,
umso besser werden die Ergebnisse.
Michael Friedel

Nature photography isn't a game of roulette
with which you capture the moment of moments.
The more you plan, the more accurately you
work, the better the results will be.
Michael Friedel

White Storks

Weißstörche

Drei Geschichten kann man zu diesen Bildern erzählen.
Die erste handelt von den Störchen: Vier Nester auf
Pfählen standen ihnen rund um den Bauernhof zur Verfü-
gung. Sie wählten dieses, das direkt an einer von über
1.000 Autos täglich benutzten Strasse lag. Warum wohl? Sie
hätten leicht eines der anderen, ruhiger gelegenen Nester
beziehen können.

Die zweite handelt von Menschen: Der Bauer bekam einen
Brief von der Behörde, ob er denn eine Baugenehmigung
für die Horstanlage hätte? Vom Straßenverkehrsamt die
Anfrage, ob auch die vorgeschriebene Distanz zur Straße
eingehalten worden wäre? Vom Bauamt die Anfrage, ob
schon eine Statikberechnung eines Ingenieurs vorliegt, und
vom Umweltamt die Anfrage, ob er auch alle Batterien und
Akkus aus dem Trabbi ausgebaut hätte. Modernes Leben...
Die dritte ist eine fotografische: Das Bild sieht nach einem
leicht und problemslos – so quasi im Vorbeigehen – ge-
machten Schnappschuß aus. In Wirklichkeit mußte ich
genau planen: Von meinem Heimatort bis zum Storchennest
waren es exakt 483 Kilometer. Für das Bild brauchte ich
blauen Himmel ohne Wolken, Wind aus Süden oder Sü-
dosten und Sonne zwischen 13.00 und 15.00 Uhr. Es hieß
also wochenlang die Wetterberichte für Neuruppin bei
Berlin genau zu verfolgen, um den idealen Tag nicht zu
verpassen.

Three stories can be told about these pictures.
The first one is about Storks: Four nests on posts stood
around the farm at their disposal. They chose the one, which
lay near a street used by 1,000 cars a day. How come? They
could have easily inhabited other, quieter nests.

The second one is about people: The farmer received a let-
ter from the authorities; did he have the construction permit for the aviary (eyrie)? From the traffic department came
the request, if the prescribed distance from the street was
being upheld.

From the construction department came the request, if an
engineer's static-calculation existed, and from the department for the environment the request, if he had removed
all the batteries and charging devices from the Trabbi (Tra-
bant). Modern life...

The third is picturesque: The photograph looks like an easy
and problem-free, so to say "in – passing" taken snapshot.
In reality I had to plan it perfectly: from my home town to
the storks´ nest it is exactly 483 kilometers; sky without
clouds, south or southeasterly wind and sun between 1:00
and 3:00PM; of course that meant weeks of following the
weather reports specifically out of Neuruppin near Berlin,
so as not to miss the perfect day.

Objectiv 4.0/400 mm, Sensia-100, Stativ-tripod. Neuruppin, Germany

Wer sehen kann, kann auch fotografieren.
Sehen lernen kann allerdings lange dauern.

Those who can see can take photographs,
but learning how to see could take a long time.

Tough Life

Hartes Leben

aiserpinguine sind die härtesten Vögel der Welt. Kein anderer Vogel ist so verrückt, bei 60 Grad Celsius minus und 24 Stunden völliger Dunkelheit am Tage, ein Ei auszubrüten, das man dabei auch noch auf den eigenen Füßen balanciert. Im letzten Licht des Herbstes, vor der großen Winterdunkelheit, legt das Weibchen ein einzelnes Ei, um danach im offenen Meer zu verschwinden. Das Männchen balanciert nun zwei Monate lang dieses Ei auf seinen Füßen durch die bittere Kälte des Winters. Das Männchen bleibt dabei etwa neunzig Tage ohne Nahrung. Erst wenn das Junge schlüpft, kehrt die Mutter vom Meer zurück.

Die Jungen wachsen zuerst langsam, wenn aber im antarktischen Frühsommer die Nahrung reichlicher wird, werden sie häufiger gefüttert und wachsen schneller. Im Alter von 5 Monaten müssen sie dann das Meer aufsuchen, weil die Eltern die Brutkolonie einen Monat vorher verlassen haben.

Erfreulich für die Pinguine ist, das es keine Landraubtiere gibt: keine Polarbären, keine Eisfüchse, nichts. Daher haben sie auch keine Angst vor Menschen. Wenn man still stehen bleibt, kommen sie in Gruppen von 2 bis 20 Exemplaren bis auf einen Meter herangelaufen, um sich diese 'unbekannten Riesenpinguine' aus der Nähe anzusehen.

Emperor penguins are the toughest birds in the world. No other bird is crazy enough to hatch their one egg, balancing it on their own feet, at 60° C below freezing and 24 hours of complete darkness.

During the last light of autumn, just before the great winter darkness, the female lays a single egg and disappears immediately into the open sea. The male will balance this egg for two months on his feet and through the bitter cold of winter. The male will be without nourishment for about 90 days. The mother won't return from the open sea until the young has hatched.

At first the youngsters will grow slowly, but when nourishment will be replenished in the early Antarctic summer and their feeding increases, they will grow faster. At the age of 5 months they have to go into the sea, because the parents will have left the breeding colony a month prior.

Happily for the penguins there are no predators for them on land, no polar bears, no arctic foxes, none. That explains why they have no fear of humans. If you stand still, they will walk up to you in groups of 2 to 20 as close as one meter in order to take a closer look at these "giant penguins".

Objectiv 2.8/80-200 mm, Sensia-100, Stativ-tripod. Dawson-Lambton-Gletscher, Antarktis

Bereit sein ist viel, warten können
ist mehr, doch den rechten
Augenblick zu nutzen ist alles.

Arthur Schnitzler

To be ready is much, to be able to wait
is much more, but to use the right moment
is everything.

Arthur Schnitzler

Der magische Moment

That Magic Moment

Aktionsfotografie gegenüber habe ich immer etwas ambivalente Gefühle.

Sie kommen beim Betrachter meistens gut an, und wenn sie gut sind, sind sie emotional. Aber – es gibt nur den einen, magischen Moment. Wenn man ihn verpaßt – Endsville. Er kommt niemals wieder.

Daher liebe ich eigentlich mehr die Nahfotografie in der Natur. Man hat hierbei alle Zeit der Welt und kann ein Bild weitgehend nach seinen Vorstellungen gestalten, was in der Aktionsfotografie nur sehr eingeschränkt möglich ist.

Hier bei diesem Bild war ich auf Sealion Island auf den Falkland Inseln und sah diesen kleinen Einfarb-Uferwipper zwischen den See-Elefanten laufen und deren Körper nach Parasiten absuchen. Plötzlich stand er vor einem dieser Kolosse und wollte Parasiten an seiner Nase abpicken. Es war plötzlich einer dieser Momente da, auf den wir Naturfotografen ja immer warten und nach dem wir suchen, der magische Qualitäten hat.

Ganz klar, dies war die klassische David und Goliath-Situation, komprimiert als Bildaussage auf den Punkt.

Nichts fehlte und nichts war zu viel da um abzulenken, und das Bild zu verwässern oder geschwätzig zu machen.

Fünf Sekunden – dann war alles vorbei, aber der emotionale und magische Moment war festgehalten.

I have always had mixed emotions, regarding action photography,

They are always well received by the viewer, and if they are good they are emotional. But – there is only one magic moment. If you miss it – Endsville. It will never come again.

That is why I love nature photography in the wild. You have, with that, all the time in the world and can create a picture largely according to your own perception, which is very limited in action photography.

In this picture I was on Sealion Island of the Falkland Islands and saw this little Tussac bird walking between the Southern Elephant Seal searching their bodies for parasites. Suddenly he stood in front of this colossus and wanted to pick parasites on his nose. Surprisingly it was just one of those moments, yes, the kind we nature photographers are always waiting and searching for, with magical qualities.

Of course, this was the classic David and Goliath situation, compressed into a fitting visual expression. Nothing missing and not too much distraction there to dilude or make the picture cluttered.

Five seconds – then it was all over, but the emotional and magical moment was captured.

Objectiv 4.0/300 mm, Kodachrome-64, Stativ-tripod.Sealion Island, Falklands

Krokodile

Crocodiles

Intelligenz ist relativ. Krokodile sind – menschlich gesehen – sicher nicht sonderlich intelligent, aber existieren schon rund 60 Millionen Jahre. Uns Menschen gibt es erst seit etwa 100.000 Jahren, aber ob wir auch nur die nächsten 1.000 Jahre überstehen – mit all unserer Intelligenz – ist fraglich.

Im Pantanal haben die zur Krokodilfamilie gehörenden Kaimane gelernt das es sich lohnt, in der Abenddämmerung mit aufgerissenem Maul an den Stromschnellen zu liegen und auf vorbeischwimmende Fische zu warten.

Komisch – anscheinend nur in Südamerika haben die Schmetterlinge entdeckt, das in der Tränenflüssigkeit um die Augen der Krokodile interessante Falternahrung enthalten ist. Auf keinem anderen Kontinent habe ich dieses Verhalten bisher gesehen. Hauptziel der Schmetterlinge ist die Flüssigkeit um die Augen, aber sie besuchen auch Nase und Zähne. Fantastisch: Ein Schmetterling kann ein Krokodil in die Flucht schlagen: Ich habe schon beobachtet, das ein Kaiman völlig genervt ins Wasser ging, wenn ein Schmetterling zu lange an seinen Augen 'herummachte'.

Um beim rechts stehenden Bild das Wasser attraktiv wiederzugeben, braucht man eine lange Verschlußzeit, was dem Naturfotografen technisch gesehen sehr entgegenkommt, weil in der Stunde zwischen Tag und Traum das Licht sowieso knapp ist.

Intelligence is relative. Crocodiles are – from a human aspect – not especially intelligent, yet they have been in existence for about 60 million years. We, the human species, in comparison only about 100.000 years and if we will survive even the next 1.000 years – with all our intelligence – is questionable. The caimans in Pantanal, a member of the crocodile family, have learned that it is quite worthwhile to lie at the foot of the rapids with open jaws when the sun is getting ready to set and wait for the passing fish. Oddly enough – apparently only in South America – have butterflies discovered that the crocodile tears around the eyes contain interesting nourishment for them. I have not been able to observe any similar behavior from butterflies on any other continent. The primary goal for butterflies is the fluid around the eyes, but they also tend to visit the nose and teeth. Fantastic – a butterfly can drive a crocodile to flee: I have seen a caiman glide into the water, completely annoyed by a butterfly that was constantly messing with his eyes. In order to have the water appear in an attractive manner in the picture to your right, you need to use a slower shutter speed, which technically speaking works in favor of the nature photographer, if you take into consideration that the hour between day and dream has such scant light in any case.

▲ Brillenkaiman & Fackelschmetterling, Yacare Caiman & Flambeau Butterfly, Objectiv 4.0/500 mm, Sensia-100, Stativ-tripod,
▶ Objectiv 2.8/100 mm, Kodachrome-200, Autostativ – Stativ-tripod. Pantanal, Brazil

**Mein Herz ist gefangen und inspiriert
von der Stille und Ruhe in der Natur**
Hazbat Inhayat Khma

**My heart is captured and inspired
by the stillness and peace of nature.**
Hazbat Inhayat Khma

Bei Sonnenaufgang

Fünf Tage hintereinander mußte ich jeden Morgen um 4.45 Uhr aufstehen, um gegen 5.15 Uhr zum eine Stunde von der Hazienda entfernt gelegenen Jaribunest zu fahren, bis der Himmel ein Einsehen hatte und ein Morgenrot spendierte. Silhouetten fotografiert man dann am sichersten mit einer manuellen Belichtungssteuerung. Denn je nach dem wie groß das eigentliche Motiv abgebildet wird, ändert sich durch die mehr oder weniger große Dominanz der schwarzen Fläche die Belichtung. Je mehr schwarze Flächen je größer abgebildet werden, je länger wird die Belichtungszeit. Wenn man also drei verschiedene Bildausschnitte nimmt und mit irgendeiner automatischen Mehrfeld- oder Integralmessung arbeitet, dann wir der Himmel im Bild heller, je größer die Silhouetten im Bild dargestellt werden. Das ist verständlich: Je mehr Schwarzanteil im Bild, je dunkler ist es draußen (meint der Belichtungsmesser) und je länger belichtet er 'gegen die Dunkelheit an'. Daher sollte man solche diffizilen Motive nicht der Kameraautomatik überlassen, sondern selber (belichtungsmäßig) in die Hand nehmen.
Bewährt hat sich folgender Weg: Man mißt neben dem Hauptmotiv mit Spotmessung den Himmel an, und öffnet um eine Blendenstufe. Wenn also der rote Himmel Blende 5.6 und 1/30 sek. anzeigt, dann stellt man manuell auf Blende 5.6 und 1/15 sek. ein.

Five days in a row I had to get up every morning at 4.45 AM, to drive at around 5.15 AM to Jaribunest, which was located an hour away from the Hacienda, until finally the heavens agreed and provided an orange sunrise.
Silhouettes are best photographed with a manual exposure setting. Then depending on how large the actual subject to be photographed is, the more or less dominant amount of black area for exposure changes. The more black area, proportionally to be photographed, the longer the exposure time should be. If you take three different parts of a picture and use any automatic multiple-field or integrated measurement, then the sky in view will become lighter and lighter, proportionally, to the silhouettes in the picture.
It is understandable: the blacker the portion in view, the darker it is outside (says the light meter) and the longer it "exposes to the darkness". That's why you shouldn't leave it to the automatics of the camera to take such difficult pictures, instead take things into your own hands (exposure-wise).
The following method has proven itself: You measure next to your subject with a spot-meter against the sky, and open one aperture setting. If the red sky aperture setting shows 5.6 and 1/30 sec., then you manually set the aperture to 5.6 and 1/15 sec.

Objectiv 4.0/500 mm, 4.0/70-200 mm, Fuji Sensia-100, Stativ – tripod. Pantanal, Brasil

Fliegende Banane

Flying Banana

Fotografien überschreiten alle Sprachbarrieren; sie können von jedem und allen unabhängig von Muttersprache und Fähigkeit zu lesen genossen werden.
Heather Angel

Photographs cross all language barriers; they can be enjoyed by everyone and anyone, independent of native language or the ability to read.
Heather Angel

Die Vogelwelt in Südamerika ist unglaublich: Wenn man zum ersten Male einen Riesentukan mit seinem Bananenschnabel vor dem strahlend blauen Himmel durch die Luft fliegen sieht – man glaubt es nicht.

Dieser hier kam jeden Morgen in den Park um die Poseida Caiman am Rande des Pantanal's geflogen um zu zu kontrollieren, ob hoch in den Bäumen über Nacht wieder einige Papayafrüchte reif geworden waren. Wenn nicht, flog er nach wenigen Minuten davon; wenn doch, hackte er sie auf und bediente sich. Am oberen Bildrand in der Mitte kann man schemenhaft einige hängen sehen.

Aber für gute Fotos war er immer zu hoch im Baum und hielt sich auch zu kurz dort auf. Daher durchschnitten wir eine Papaya und klemmten sie in halber Höhe des Baumes in eine Astgabel. Jetzt bauten wir in etwa zehn Meter Entfernung ein Tarnzelt auf, und ich setzte mich eine Stunde vor der geschätzen Ankunft des Riesentukans am Morgen hinein und harrte der Dinge, die da vielleicht kommen würden. Es war unglaublich: Er kam, sah die aufgeschnittene Papaya und und flog sofort zu ihr und bediente sich. Nicht nur Liebe geht durch den Magen...

Zum Glück schien so früh am Morgen keine Sonne, wodurch die Farben im Bild besser kommen und das Foto wunderbar harmonisch wirkt. Sonnenflecken hätten es zerrissen und unruhig erscheinen lassen.

The world of birds in South America is unbelievable: the first time you see a giant toucan with its banana beak flying through the air in front of a clear blue sky – you just can't believe it.

This one came flying around the Poseida Caiman at the edge of the Pantanal into the park to check if, high among the trees, during the night another papaya fruit had ripened. If there wasn't one he would fly away after a few minutes; if he did find one he hacked it open and served himself. You can see the silhouette of some hanging there at the edge of the upper portion of the picture.

But he was always too high up in the tree for any good pictures and did not stay there very long. That is why we cut a papaya in half and stuck them about half way up a trunk into the fork of a tree. Then we built a camouflage tent at a distance of approx. 10 meters and I took my position inside an hour before the time we thought the giant toucan would arrive in the morning and just waited for whatever was about to happen. It was amazing: he came, saw the cut open papaya, flew to it and served himself. Not only love makes its way through the stomach....

Luckily the sun was not shining that early in the morning which enabled the colors to come out better and brought a harmonious effect to the picture. Sunspots would have made it appear restless and cut up.

Objectiv 4.0/500 mm & 1.4x Converter, Sensia-100, Stativ – tripod, Pantanal, Brasil

Das Leben eines Naturfotografen
ist nicht einfach, aber –
einer muß es ja machen…

The life of a nature photographer
is not easy, but –
somebody has to do it…

Enchanted Islands

Verzauberte Inseln

Vielleicht ist der Vulkan Alcedo auf den Galapagos Inseln der einzige Platz auf der Welt, wo man Galapagos-Bussarde auf dem Rücken von Elefantenschildkröten sehen kann. Tui de Roy hatte das schon vor mir fotografiert, ebenso Udo Hirsch und Tjitte de Vries. Dieses Verhalten ist nicht die Regel, kommt aber doch so häufig vor, das man es nicht eine Rarität nennen kann. Nur junge Bussarde tun es, ebenso wie nur junge Schneeaffen mit Schneebällen spielen. Ich habe nie einen alten Bussard auf einer Schildkröte landen sehen, weder persönlich noch auf Fotos von Kollegen.

Es ist sicher Neugier und Unbekümmertheit. Auf und in den Vulkan Alcedo kommen jährlich nur so etwa 10-20 Menschen, und das ist anscheinend eine willkommene Abwechslung für die jungen Bussarde. Sie kommen dann oft vom gegenüberliegenden Kraterrand über Kilometer angeflogen, wenn sie Menschen oben wandern sehen und landen dann irgendwo in der Nähe. Und da Bäume sehr rar sind, und die bei Bussarden ja außerordentlich beliebten Weidenpfähle hier oben völlig fehlen, darf es halt' auch mal eine Schildkröte sein.

Wie mir Freunde auf Galapagos erzählten, kamen Mitte des letzten Jahrhunderts, als die ersten Menschen auf dem Alcedo mit seinen 3.000 Schildkröten zelteten, manchmal bis zu 100 Bussarde angeflogen.

Perhaps the Alcedo Volcano on the Galapagos Islands is the only place where you can observe the buzzard-like Galapagos hawk on the back of a giant tortoise.
Tui de Roy had photographed this before I did, as did Udo Hirsch and Tjitte de Vries. This type of behavior is not normal but does happen often enough for it not to be considered a rarity. Only the young birds do this, just like only young snow monkeys form snowballs for play. Personally I have never seen an older hawk land on the back of a tortoise nor have I seen pictures of it from colleagues.

Surely it must be curiosity and carefreeness. Only 10-20 people come to or go onto the Alcedo Volcano per year, so this seems to be a welcome distraction for the young hawks. When they see people hiking on the edge of the crater they often come flying from the opposite edge, across numerous kilometers and land somewhere close by. Since trees are a rarity and the fence poles so well liked by hawks are not in existence here, a tortoise will have to do. My friends on Galapagos told me that in the middle of last year, when the first people went on top of Alcedo with its 3000 tortoises, sometimes up to 100 hawks came flying up.

Objectiv 4.0/200 mm, Kodachrome-64, Freihandaufnahme – handheld, Alcedo Volcano , Galapagos Islands

Wunder

Miracles

Als vor 130 bis 140 Millionen Jahre die Blütenpflanzen unseren Planeten 'betraten', kamen auch die ersten Schmetterlinge. Inzwischen sind rund 170.000 Schmetterlingsarten entdeckt und beschrieben worden.

Aber keine Art hat uns Menschen so überrascht wie der Monarchfalter. Erst 1976 entdeckte der kanadische Schmetterlingsforscher Fred Urquart, daß der Monarch die Winter in Mexikos Hochgebirge verbringt, in riesigen Kolonien in 3.000 bis 4.000 Meter Höhe. Dieser nur wenige Zentimeter große Falter fliegt von den Seen im Süden Kanadas und den USA jeden Herbst viele tausend Kilometer bis in die Wälder des mexikanischen Bundesstaates Michoacan.

Niemand weiß bis jetzt ganz genau, wie er sich dabei orientiert, man vermutet an Magnetfeldern. Er startet zu dem langen Flug in kleinen Verbänden, wobei er widrigen Luftströmungen ausweicht. Bei Gegenwind fliegen diese Gruppen dicht über dem Boden, aber bei Rückenwind steigen sie hoch über die Wolken – dahin, wo die Freiheit wohl grenzenlos ist – und man hat Monarchverbände schon in über 2.500 Meter Höhe beobachtet. 10.000 Falter am blauen Himmel über sich fliegen zu sehen ist ein grandioses Bild. Die zehn bekanntesten Winterquartiere in Mexiko sind zu Schutzgebieten erklärt worden und bringen der Region bescheidenen Wohlstand durch einen Schmetterlingstourismus.

When the blossoming plants appeared on our planet 130 to 140 million years ago, they also brought the first butterflies. In the meantime about 170.000 types of butterflies have been discovered and recorded.

But no other has surprised us more then the monarch butterfly. Not until 1976 did the Canadian entomologist Fred Urquart discover that the monarch migrated to the Mexican highlands for the winter where they formed gigantic colonies at an altitude of 3.000 to 4.000 meters. This butterfly of a few centimeters in size flies from the Great Lakes in Southern Canada and the United Stated many thousands of kilometers during the fall until it reaches the forests of the Mexican state of Michoaoan.

Up to now no-one knows just how it gets and keeps its bearings, some presume magnetic fields. They gather in small bunches to start this long flight during which they avoid unfavorable airstreams. When they have headwinds they fly close to the ground and with backwinds they soar high above the clouds – the place where freedom seems to have no bounds – and swarms of monarch butterflies have been observed at altitudes of over 2.500 meters. To have 10.000 butterflies passing above you against the blue sky is a spectacular picture. The ten best known hibernating places have been turned into sanctuaries and bring modest prosperity to the region through the ensuing tourism.

Objectiv 4.0/70-200 mm, Sensia-100, Michoacan, Mexiko

**Am Ende schützen wir nur was wir lieben,
wir lieben nur was wir verstehen,
und wir verstehen nur war uns gelehrt wurde.**
Baba Dioum, Senegalesischer Poet

**In the final analysis we only save what we love,
we love only what we understand and
we understand only what we've been taught.**
Baba Dioum, Senegalian poet

Fischadler

Osprey

Beamte sind kreativ, spontan und fantasievoll – verglichen mit Fischadlern. Das Männchen fliegt am Morgen zwischen 8 und 9 Uhr mal eben übers Wasser, erbeutet einen Fisch, und landet damit in nicht zu großer Entfernung vom Horst um die Beute gemütlich vom Kopf her aufzuessen.

Um die vordere Hälfte des Fisches zu verzehren, läßt er sich fast eine ganze Stunde Zeit. Da kann das brütende Weibchen – und später auch die größeren Jungen – noch so laut, gellend und ausdauernd rufen, er frißt nicht schneller und kommt auch nicht eher mit dem Fisch zur Familie. Er fliegt erst zum Horst, wenn die vordere Hälfte des Fisches komplett fehlt (kleines Bild).

Was nicht so gut auf Beobachter wirkt – und uns Menschen auch etwas brutal dem noch lebenden Fisch gegeüber wirkt – ist die Tatsache, das Fischaugen wohl für den Adler eine Delikatesse sind, denn die frißt er immer zuerst.

Wenn man solche Fotos machen will, muß man nur den Baum kennen, auf dem der Fischadler zur Brutzeit mit seinem ersten Fisch am Morgen landet um ihn zu verzehren. Er wird mit Sicherheit pünktlich zwischen 8 und 9 Uhr dort ankommen, das ist er seiner Beamtenehre schuldig.

Hier hebt er die Flügel leicht an und warnt gellend einen vorbeifliegenden Kollegen, sich auf keinen Fall näher für diesen Wels zu interessieren.

State workers are creative, spontaneous and full of fantasy – when compared to ospreys. The male osprey takes the time between 8 and 9 am to fly over the water, catch a fish and land with it not too far away from his eyrie in order to eat it head first.

He takes about an hour to eat the first half of the fish. No matter how loud or long the brooding female – and then later the youngsters – cry, he does not eat any faster and will not come to the family any sooner with the fish.

He will come to the eyrie only when the entire front half of the fish is completely gone. (small picture)

This does not leave a very aesthetic impression with onlookers – and it does appear to be quite brutal on the still living fish – but the fact of the matter is, that the eyes of the fish appear to be a delicacy for the eagle since he always eats them first and foremost.

If you want to take pictures like these, you only have to know which tree the osprey uses during nesting time and takes his first fish to every morning for feeding. With certainty he will be there punctually between 8 and 9 am, something he thinks he owes to bureaucracy.

Here he is lifting his wing slightly while he screeches a warning to a colleague who is flying by, not to get too close to the catfish under any circumstances.

Objectiv 4.0/500 mm & Converter 1.4x, Sensia-100, Stativ-tripod, Sanibel Island, Florida, USA

Alligator

Alligators

**Das Schönste, was wir entdecken können,
ist das Geheimnisvolle.**
Albert Einstein

**The most beautiful thing we can discover
is the mysterious**
Albert Einstein

Bei über einer Million Exemplare brauchten die Alligatoren heute in Florida sicher nicht mehr unter Schutz zu stehen. Aber weil es gleichzeitig nur knapp eintausend Spitzkrokodile gibt, und davon ziemlich viele als Alligatoren abgeschossen würden, wenn man diese jagen dürfte, macht es schon Sinn.

Was mich immer am meisten wundert wenn ich in Florida bin und diese Echsen fotografiere, ist die Tatsache, das ich nie einen Schmetterling an ihren Augen sehe. Die fast gleich großen – und auch zur Familie gehörenden – Kaimane in Südamerika werden regelmäßig von Faltern an den Augen besucht, um in der Tränenflüssigkeit Minerale aufzunehmen. Warum tun sich wohl die Falter Nordamerikas so schwer, diese interessante Gesundheitsquelle zu entdecken?

Ein schwarzer Alligator in schwarzem Wasser ist der Traum eines jeden Naturfotografen, denn nichts versinnbildlicht mehr die dunkle, drohende Seite dieses Tieres.

Die so genannten Alligatorlöcher sind in der Trockenzeit die einzige Zuflucht für alles, was Wasser braucht. Sobald aber dann mit dem Sommerregen wieder bessere Zeiten anbrechen, breiten sich alle Tiere, welche die Gastfreundschaft der Alligatoren ungefressen überlebt haben, wieder in den Everglades aus.

At more then a million in number the alligator certainly is not in need of sanctuary in Florida any longer. On the other hand, there are only about one Thousand of the American crocodile left and of which many would be shot, mistaken as alligators, if the restrictions were lifted, which in turn gives sense to the continuing preservation.

Something that puzzles me the most when I am shooting reptiles in Florida is the fact that I don't see any butterflies around their eyes. The caimans of South America – who are part of this reptile family and similar in size – are regularly visited by butterflies who take nourishment from the tears of their eyes which contain important minerals. Why would the butterflies of North America have such problems finding this interesting fountain of health?

A black alligator in the black water is the dream of every nature photographer since there is nothing else which reflects the dark and threatening side of this animal any better.

The so-called alligator holes are the only sanctuary for everything that is in dire need of water during the drought. As soon as better times arrive, together with the summer rains, all animals that survived the hospitality of the alligators without being eaten scatter all over the Everglades again.

Objectiv 5,6/600 mm, Kodachrome-64, Stativ-tripod. Sanibel Island, Florida, USA

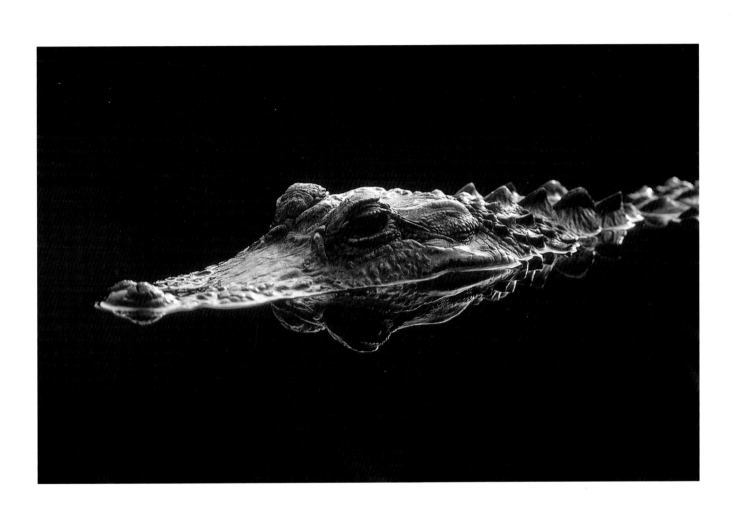

**Wenn man sich im Wald hinsetzt
und wartet – irgend etwas wird passieren.**
Henry David Thoreau

**You learn that if you sit down in the woods
and wait, something will happen.**
Henry David Thoreau

Screech owl in the jungle

Schrei-Eule im Urwald

Ordentlich, in Reih und Glied, gesund und nicht zu alt, ohne Unterholz, und außerdem möglichst nur in einer Sorte, so sollen sie im Walde stehen – die Bäume. Das ist der Traum von Holznutzern und auch – leider – immer noch von manchen Förstern. Tiere mögen das überhaupt nicht. Naturfotografen auch nicht.

Viele Pflanzen und Tiere finden ihre beste Heimat in Urwäldern, eine einmalige Kombination aus kleinen jungen und großen alten Bäumen, gefallenen Stämmen und noch stehenden, aber toten Bäumen. Dies zusammen gibt den Tieren die besten Möglichkeiten Nahrung, Schutz und Brutplätze zu finden.

In den USA sind 98 % aller Urwälder getötet worden; wenn die letzten 2 % auch noch verschwinden, hat auch die Schrei-Eule keine Heimat mehr.

Dieses Foto ist eines meiner Lieblingsbilder, weil es nicht nur das Tier zeigt, sondern vermittelt, wo es lebt und wie seine Heimat aussieht.

Es ist eine der letzten echten, tropischen Zypressen-Urwald-Gesellschaften in Nordamerika. Viele dieser Bäume standen schon da, als Kolumbus nach New York segelte. Wenn Sie einmal in Florida sind, sollten Sie diese Wildnis besuchen. Es führt ein 3.5 km langer Holzsteg durch diesen sumpfigen Urwald, und Sie werden begeistert sein.

Orderly, in rows and segments, healthy and not too old, without undergrowth and besides that only one kind if possible, that is how they should be in the forest – the trees. That is a wood cutters dream and – unfortunately also that of most forest rangers. Animals don't like this at all. Nature photographers don't either.

Many plants and animals find their best homes in jungles, a unique combination of small, young and larger, older trees, and fallen as well as still standing trunks of dead trees. These combined will provide the animals with the best possibilities for finding nourishment, safety and breeding space.

In the US 98% of the existing jungles have been killed; when the last 2% disappear, the screech owl will lose her home as well. This is one of my favorite pictures, since it does not only show the animal but conveys where it lives and what its habitat looks like. It is one of the last real tropical cypress jungles in Northern America. Many of these trees were already standing when Columbus sailed to New York. If you happen to be in Florida you should visit this wilderness. There is a 3.5 km path of wood through this swampy jungle and you will be thrilled. On its outskirts the Audubon Society has built one of the nicest visitor centers in North America.

Audubon Cork Screw Swamp Wildlife Sanctuary, Naples, Florida, USA

▶▶ *Silberreiher – Great Egret, Everglades national park, USA*

**Wir haben verlernt, die Augen auf etwas ruhen
zu lassen. Deshalb erkennen wir so wenig.**

Jean Giono

**We lost the ability of resting our eyes
on something. That is why we recognize so little.**

Jean Giono (adapted)

Antelope-Canyon

Der Puls des Lebens geht manchmal ganz schön unregelmäßig – vom absoluten Ruhezustand hinauf in rasende Höhen.

So ist ein Flußbett bei Page City in Arizona fast immer wasserlos, bis zu den Zeiten, wo es etwa im Gebirge in 50 km Entfernung wolkenbruchartig regnet. Dann wird das sandige Flußbett mit Wasser bedeckt. Dramatisch wird es nur auf 100 Meter Flußverlauf, da, wo sich vor dem gemächlich ankommenden Regenwasser plötzlich eine 10 Meter hohe Felswand aus Navajo-Sandstein auftürmt – mit nur einer 2 Meter breiten Felsspalte.

Jetzt muß sich der 20 Meter breite Fluß durch diese schmale Spalte zwängen, und dabei türmen sich die Wassermassen mit Urgewalt – und rasend schnell – im Canyon zu einer Höhe von 10 Metern auf.

Das Wasser kommt oft ohne Vorwarnung – es kann in Page City Sonnenschein und strahlend blauer Himmel sein – wenn es weit entfernt im Gebirge regnet, kommt das Unheil leise, schnell und unbemerkt. Zuletzt starben sieben Touristen 1997, die in diesem Canyon vom Wasser überrascht wurden, dessen Name auf die Sage der Indianer zurückgeht, das früher Antilopen in ihm weideten.

Bis vor einigen Jahren war er ein Geheimtipp unter Landschaftsfotografen, aber heute besuchen ihn tausende jährlich in den Sommermonaten.

The pulse of life is at times very irregular – from an extreme tranquility up to erratic heights.

There is a riverbed close to Page City in Arizona which is almost always dry except for the times when a cloudburst of rain comes down 50 km away. Then the sandy riverbed is covered with water. The dramatic part is a length of 100 meters of river where suddenly a wall of Navajo sandstone rises 10 meters up out of the ground and the water masses slowly approach this gap of only 2 meters.

That means the river which is 20 meters in width has to squeeze itself through this small opening which causes the water masses to bunch up with such great force and speed, building a wall of water 10 meters high in the canyon.

Most of the time the water comes without prior warning – the sky could be blue and the sun bright in the sky of Page City – when the rains fall in the mountains far away and disaster approaches quickly, quietly and unnoticed. In 1997, the most recent event, 7 tourists who were surprised by the water masses in the canyon died. A canyon whose name originated from a saga of the Indians, that antelopes used to graze in there.

Up to a few years ago this was a well known secret for landscape photographers, but nowadays thousands of visitors come every year during the summer months.

Objectiv 3.5-4.5/28-105 mm, Velvia-50, Stativ-tripod. Page-City, Arizona, USA

Zitat

Quote

In der Natur fühlen wir uns wohl,
weil sie kein Urteil über uns hat.
Arthur Schopenhauer

We feel comfortable in nature
because she holds no judgment over us.
Arthur Schopenhauer (adapted)

In der – mit rund 125 Jahren – noch recht jungen Geschichte der Naturfotografie, gibt es trotzdem schon einige atemberaubende Ikonen. Etwa das wahrscheinlich nie mehr besser zu fotografierende Bild von Jim Brandenburg, welches einen weißen Wolf zeigt, der auf einem Eisberg thront. Oder das unglaubliche, fast von einem anderen Planeten stammende Foto eines blauen Eisberges, auf dem eine Gruppe Pinguine sitzt und das von Cherry Alexander aufgenommen wurde. Solche Ikonen der Naturfotografie sind sicher unwiederholbar.

Es gibt aber auch einmalige und perfekte Motive, die nicht bestimmten Naturfotografen zugeschrieben werden, die aber ebenfalls Ikonen sind und von jedem wiederholt oder zitiert werden können. So ein Motiv ist Mesa Arch mit dem Island in the Sky Area im Canyonlands National Park in Utah. Es ist sicher schon von hunderten und tausenden Naturfotografen exakt so festgehalten worden, und – man kann es auch kaum besser aufnehmen.

Diese atemberaubende Landschaft mit dem Naturbogen im Vordergrund, der auf seiner Unterseite von der aufgehenden Sonne bestrahlt wird, ist ein so unglaubliches Motiv, dass man es einfach fotografieren muß, wenn man schon mal da ist. Auch wenn niemandem einfällt, wie man es besser oder anders fotografieren könnte wie die vielen, die vor einem da waren.

There are some breathtaking icons despite the relatively young history of about 125 years in nature photography. Like, for instance, the untoppable picture of Jim Brandenburg which shows a white wolf sitting majestically on an iceberg. Or the unbelievable picture that looks almost as if it was set on another planet, of a blue iceberg with a group of penguins on it, taken by Cherry Alexander. Certainly you can't take pictures like that again.

Nevertheless there are perfect and unique subjects which are accounted for by no specific nature photographer which are icons as well, but which can be repeatedly used or quoted.

Such a motif is Mesa Arch with the island in the sky area of the Canyon Lands National Park in Utah. It certainly has been captured by hundreds and thousands of nature photographers just the same and – there is no better way to shoot it.

This breathtaking landscape with the natural arch in front, which has the rising sun shining on it from below is such an unbelievable motif that you just have to take a picture of it when you are there. Even if there is no better or different way of shooting it, then what most others who were there before you did.

46
47

Objectiv 3.5-4.5/20-35 mm, Fujichrome Velvia-50, Stativ – tripod. Canyonlands National Park, USA

Licht ist alles

Light is Everything

**Das Auge macht das Bild,
nicht die Kamera.**
Gisele Freund

**The eye takes the picture,
not the camera.**
Gisele Freund

Wenn ich die Qual der Wahl hätte zwischen Tierfotografie, Landschaftsfotografie und Nahfotografie, würde ich immer die Nahfotografie wählen. Sie ist ohne Zweifel der angenehmste Part in der Naturfotografie. In der Tierfotografie muß man oft Stunden warten, bevor etwas passiert, das ein Foto zu machen lohnt. In der Landschaftsfotografie hängt (fast) alles vom Licht ab. Man muß oft tagelang warten, bis die Lichtstimmung plötzlich da ist, die dem Motiv angemessen scheint.

Nahfotografie ist die entspannendste Art zu fotografieren: Man sieht ein Motiv – ein Pilz, ein Blatt, eine Struktur – und fotografiert es. Wenn man Licht braucht und die Sonne scheint nicht, dann hellt man auf. Und wenn das Sonnenlicht zu hart ist, dann nimmt man eben den Softschirm. Es gibt keine Wartezeiten die einen verzweifeln lassen wie in der Tier- und Landschaftsfotografie. Man macht einfach sein Foto und wandert frohgemut weiter – herrlich.

Ganz besonders schlimm sind in der Landschaftsfotografie Motive die kategorisch eine ganz spezielle Lichtstimmung verlangen, und diese dann auch noch nur für wenige Minuten am Tage herrscht. So gibt es etwa am Strand des Acadia Nationalparks in Nordamerika für dieses Motiv nur 5 Minuten Licht direkt bei Sonnenaufgang und man braucht – natürlich – mindesten 5 Tage, um einmal dieses traumhafte Licht zu bekommen. Dr. Murphys Gesetz…

If I had to make the painful decision between wildlife photography, landscape photography and close-up photography I would choose the close-up photography each and every time. This is without a doubt the most agreeable part of nature photography. With wildlife photography you will often have to spend many hours with waiting before something happens which is worth taking a picture of. When it comes to landscape photography it (everything just about) depends on the light. Sometimes you have to wait for days for the light conditions to be seemingly suitable. Close-up is the most relaxed type of photography: you see a subject – a mushroom, a leaf, a structure – and you take a picture of it. If you need light and the sun is not shining, you lighten it. If the sunshine is too harsh, you take the softening screen. There are no waiting periods filling you with despair as in wildlife or landscape photography. You just take your picture and happily move on – wonderful.

Especially difficult are landscapes that categorically require special light conditions which, on top of it all, are only available for a few minutes during the day.

For instance on the beach of the Acadia National Park in Northern America, where there are only five minutes directly after sun-up to take a picture of this specific subject and – of course – you need 5 days for the opportunity of having this wonderful light just once. Dr. Murphy's law…

Objectiv 3.5-4.5/20-35 mm, Fujichrome Velvia-50, Stativ – tripod. Acadia National Park, USA

In einem glücklichen Moment kann sich in der Naturfotografie die Redlichkeit des fotografischen Handwerks mit der Kühnheit der Kunst und der Spekulation der Philosophie verbinden.

During a lucky moment in nature photography the honesty of the photographic work can be connected to the boldness of art and the speculation of philosophy

Starfish

Seesterne

Im felsigen Uferbereich Seesterne zu fotografieren ist nicht ganz einfach, obwohl sie bewegungslos an den Steinen festgeklammert sitzen. Erstens sind nur die unfotogenen leicht im Ebbe- und Flutbereich zu finden. Die tollen sitzen natürlich immer ganz weit draußen. Dann findet man sie auch – fast – immer im verblauenden Schatten und – natürlich – an einer senkrechten, und nicht waagerechten Felswand. Aber manchmal hat man Glück und findet – wie hier – freundliche Seesterne, leicht erreichbar auf einem kleinen, waagerechten Stein in der Uferzone.

Hier hatte ich nun die Gelegenheit, die Statik der sich an den Felsen anklammernden Tiere durch die Bewegung des fließenden Wassers aufzulösen, und durch eine Zeitbelichtung beides in einen reizvollen Kontrast zu bringen um gleichzeitig zu zeigen, wie sich Seesterne verhalten und mit der aufkommenden Flut leben.

Da die Wellen immer sehr schnell kamen und auch mit großem Druck, arbeitete ich mit einer Belichtungszeit von 1 Sekunde, da mir bei noch längeren Zeiten das Wasser zu weiß geworden wäre und seinen Bezug zur Realität verloren hätte.

Hier im Olympic Nationalpark in der Nähe von Seattle leben an der Küstenlinie fantastische Seesterne und anderes Getier der Uferzone. Es ist ein Paradies für Freunde der Natur und auch ein Schlaraffenland für Fotografen.

To photograph starfish on the rocky shores is not easy, even though they are sitting, clinging motionless, tightly to the rocks.

First, only the non-photogenic are found easily in the ebb and neap tide area. Naturally the pretty ones are always very far out. And then one can also find them (almost) always in the bluing shadow and (naturally) on a vertical not horizontal wall of rock. But sometimes you get lucky – like here – and find friendly starfish, easily accessible on a small stone laying flat on the shoreline.

Here I had the opportunity to ease the static of these animals that cling to rocks through the movement of water, and capture both, through a timed-exposure, in an attractive contrast, in order to show simultaneously how starfish relate and live with the rising tide.

Since the waves always came very quickly and with extreme power, I worked with a shutter speed of 1 second, because the water would have turned too white with longer exposure times and the sense of reality would have been lost.

Here in the Olympic National Park, close to Seattle, fantastic starfish and other creatures live along the coastline. It is a paradise for friends of nature and also "a land of milk and honey" for photographers.

Objectiv 2.8/105 mm, Sensia-100, Stativ-tripod, Olympic National Park, USA

**Alles was gegen die Natur ist,
hat auf Dauer keinen Bestand.**
Charles Darwin

**Everything that goes against nature
can not exist for long.**
Charles Darwin (adapted)

Kojoten

Coyotes

Wer im Sommer in den ältesten Nationalpark der Welt kommt und sich 'falsch' verhält, der findet ihn völlig überfüllt.

Aber – von den drei Millionen Besucher verlassen nur 1 % die Autostrassen und benutzen Wanderwege. Wer also ungestört sein möchte, kann das ganz leicht, wenn er sich ein bisschen bewegt.

Noch besser ist es im Winter: Nur 3 % der Yellowstone-Besucher kommen zur kalten Jahreszeit in den Park. Er ist dann für Autos geschlossen, und man bewegt sich zu Fuß, auf Skiern, mit Schneemobilen oder Schneecoaches.

Für viele Naturfreunde ist der Winter im Yellowstone besonders attraktiv, wegen der um 1995 wieder eingeführten Wölfe. Seit es die wieder gibt, ist allerdings die Population der Kojoten um 50 % zurückgegangen.

Manchmal profitieren sie aber auch von den Wölfen. Hier sieht man einen Kojoten an einem Wolfskill, einem Wapiti, dessen Reste jetzt dem Kojoten zugute kommen.

Im Lamar Tal hat man seit einigen Jahren ziemlich gute Chancen, Wölfe zu beobachten. Der beste Platz auf der ganzen Welt um mit ziemlicher Sicherheit freilebende Wölfe zu sehen, ist die Strasse von Mammot Hot Springs nach Cooke City in der letzten Mai- und der ersten Juniwoche, wenn dort viele Tiere ihre Jungen bekommen und die Wölfe und Bären reiche Beute machen.

Those who come to the oldest national park in the world and don't know how to act will find it overly crowded.

From the three Million visitors only 1% leave the paved streets and use the hiking trails. So those of you who do want to be undisturbed can be, if you just exercise a little. It is even better in the winter season. Only 3% of the Yellowstone visitors come to the park during the colder parts of the year. The park is closed for cars at that time and you have to move on foot, on skis, with snow mobiles or snow coaches.

The winter is especially attractive for nature-lovers because of the wolves that were reintroduced to this area in 1995. Since the return of the wolves the coyote population has shrunk by 50%. There are times, however, when the coyotes profit from the wolves. Here you see a coyote at the site of a wolfs kill, a wapiti, the remains of which are now the benefit of the coyote.

The best chance in the past few years of catching sight of a wolf is in the Lamar Valley. The best spot in the whole world to surely observe actually free-living wolves is the street from Mammoth Hot Springs to Cooke City during the last week of May and the first week in June. That is when most of the animals bear their young and wolves and bears alike find a multitude of prey.

Objectiv 4.0/500 mm, Converter 1.4x, Sensia-100, Stativ-tripod, Yellowstone Nationalpark, USA

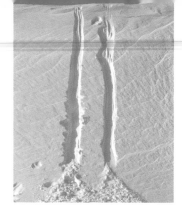

Wildnis ist eine Absage
an die Arroganz des Menschen
Aldo Leopold

Wilderness is a renunciation
of the arrogance of man
Aldo Leopold

Polar bears

Eisbären

Am Wapusk Nationalpark (Weißer Bär Nationalpark) in der Nähe von Churchill in Manitoba, Kanada, verlassen Anfang März die Eisbärinnen mit den Kleinen ihre Höhlen. Manchmal sieht man sie dann noch einige Tage vor der Höhle in einem Tagesbett liegen, wie auf dem kleinen Bild oben rechts.

Diese Jungen sind Ende Januar, Anfang Februar in der Höhle, tief unter Schnee begraben, zur Welt gekommen, und waren da nicht viel mehr als rattengroß. Jetzt im März schon wandern sie mit der Mutter zur Hudson Bay, die Nahrung verspricht, nachdem die Bärin viele Monate gefastet hatte. Im Oktober/November dann sind die Jungen schon deutlich gewachsen, und man kann sie mit der Mutter zusammen aus den Tundra Buggys bei Churchill, der 'Welthauptstadt der Eisbären' beobachten, im Alter von dann neun bis zehn Monaten.

Eisbären bleiben lange 'an den Rockschößen von Mama' hängen, wie das untere Bild zeigt. Hier sind die Kinder schon erwachsen, aber immer noch in Begleitung ihrer Mutter.

Normalerweise löst sich der Familienverbund nach 1.5 bis 2.5 Jahre auf, und die Jungen beginnen ein eigenes, selbständiges Leben zu führen.

Churchill in Manitoba ist der beste Platz auf der ganzen Welt, um im Oktober/November mit Sicherheit und auch relativ ungefährdet, Eisbären beobachten zu können.

In the Wapusk National park (white bear national park) in the area of Churchill, Manitoba, Canada, the female polar bears leave their lair in the beginning of March. At times you can observe them for a few days at the entrance of their cave in a type of day-bed, as seen in the small picture in the upper right hand. These cubs were born in the cave buried deep under the snow at the end of January / beginning February, no bigger then the size of a rat. Now, in March, they are all ready to journey with their mom to the Hudson Bay which promises food in abundance for the female bear after many months of hibernation. By October / November the cubs have visibly grown and you can see them at the age of nine to ten months from the tundra-buggies, together with their mother, in the area of Churchill, the "polar bear capitol of world".

Polar bears "pull on momma's apron strings" for quite some time, as seen in the picture below. There you see them fully grown, but still in the company of their mother.

Normally the family ties dissolve after 1.5 to 2.5 years and the cubs begin to lead their own and independent life.

Churchill in Manitoba is the greatest place in the world where you can be certain to see polar bears during the months of October / November and to observe them in relative safety.

Objectiv 4.0/500 mm, Sensia-100, Stativ-tripod, Churchill, Manitoba, Canada

Bald Eagle

Weisskopfseeadler

Menschen helfen gerne Tieren über den Winter. Die Jäger richten Futterstellen ein für das Wild. Vogelschützer in Nordeuropa legen tote Schweine aus für die Adler oder präparieren Äcker mit Nahrung für die rastenden Kraniche und Gänse. Der Einzelmensch hilft mit Futterhäuschen auf dem Balkon oder im Garten.

Aber was Jean Keene, die 'Eagle Lady' von Homer in Alaska macht, ist wohl einmalig in der Welt.
Sie lebt im Hafen von Homer und füttert in den Wintermonaten bis zu 300 freilebende Weisskopfseeadler. Jeden Morgen um Punkt 9.00 Uhr verteilt sie vor ihrem Wohnwagen etwa einen Zentner Fischabfälle aus einer nahe gelegenen Fischfabrik an die Adler.
Dann kommen die Greifvögel aus den berühmten 'allen Himmelsrichtungen' angeflogen um sich ihren Anteil an der Mahlzeit zu sichern. Manchmal gibt es natürlich Streit untereinander, und auch die Möwen und Krähen versuchen sich einen Anteil an der Nahrung zu sichern.
Diese Adler sind im Laufe der Jahre so 'zahm' an diesem Platz geworden, dass sich Menschen ihnen bis auf wenige Meter nähern können. Auch bleiben viele von ihnen den ganzen Tag im Hafen sitzen – bis zur nächsten Fütterung – so das es wohl im Winter auf der ganzen Welt keinen Hafen gibt, in dem man so viele Seeadler sitzen und fliegen sehen kann wie hier.

Humans like to help animals get through the winter. Rangers set up feeding grounds for game. Northern European bird lovers put out dead pigs for the eagles or prepare fields with nourishment for the geese and cranes that stop to rest. People in every day life help with bird houses on the balcony or in the garden.
On the other hand, what Jean Keene, the "Eagle Lady" in Homer, Alaska does is certainly unique all over the world. She lives in the harbor of Homer and feeds up to 300 wild bald eagles throughout the winter months. Every morning at exactly 9am she scatters about a hundred pounds of fish cuttings from a nearby fish factory for the eagles.
That is when the great birds of prey come from every point of the compass to secure their portion of the meal. Sometimes a fight will break out among them and of course the seagulls and crows will try to grab a piece of the food as well.
At that location these eagles have become so "tame" throughout the years, that humans can get as close as just a few meters in distance to them. Some will even spend the rest of the day in the harbor, sitting there and waiting for the next feeding. There doesn't seem to be another place in the world where you can see so many great eagles sit or fly throughout the winter, as there in that little harbor.

Objectiv 4.0/400 mm, Sensia-100, Stativ-tripod. Homer, Alaska, USA

Ocean

Ozean

In einem Meer aus Vermilion Sandstein liegt ein winziges Gebiet, 'Die Welle' genannt, das heute ein 'berühmter Geheimtipp' ist. Es liegt an der Strasse zwischen Page und Kanab in Utah, im Paria Vermilion Cliffs Wilderness Area, am Grand Staircase Escalante National Monument, und ist (Vorsicht) von berauschender Wirkung für Naturfotografen. Daher darf man es auch nur mit Genehmigung (Permit) besuchen.

Objectiv 4.0/17-40 mm, Fujichrome Velvia-50, Pol-Filter, Stativ - tripod.

There is a teeny-tiny area in an ocean of Vermillion Sandstone called „The Wave" which is a well known insiders tip nowadays. You will find it by the road that leads between Page and Kanab in Utah in the Pariah Vermilion Cliffs wilderness Area at the Grand Staircase Escalante National Monument and has a (careful!) intoxicating effect on nature photographers. That is why you need a permit to visit there.

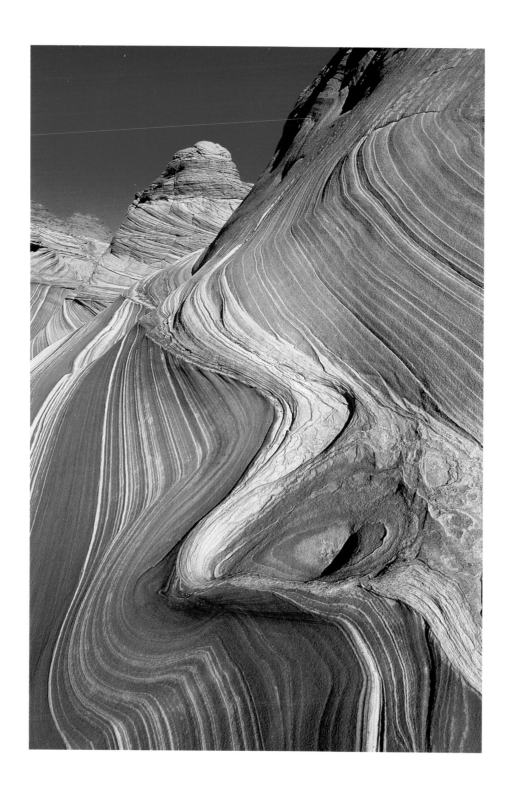

Walrosse

Walrus

**Naturfotografie kann Fotojournalismus sein,
Kunst, Kamerajagd, Wissenschaft
oder Manipulation.**

**Nature photography can be photo journalism,
art, photo shoot, science
or manipulation.**

Im Gewässer vor dem Jakeman-Gletscher von Ellesmere Island schwimmen auch im Sommer kleine und größere Eisschollen, auf denen sich manchmal Walrosse ausruhen. Dies zu wissen und hinzukommen sind allerdings zwei Paar Schuhe. Zuerst muß man nach Winnipeg in Kanada und von dort weiter zur Resolute Bay, dem nördlichsten Punkt, der noch von Linienmaschinen angeflogen wird.

Dort heißt es warten, bis eine kleine Fokker zu den Eskimosiedlungen auf Ellesmere Island fliegt. Von dort geht es mit einem kleinen Boot mit Außenbordmotor weiter zum Jakeman-Gletscher. Dort übernachtet man in mitgebrachten Zelten und sucht tagsüber mit dem Boot die See nach Eisschollen ab und entdeckt dann mit Glück irgendwann eine mit Walrossen. Mit abgestelltem Motor läßt man sich dann vorsichtig und paddelnd herantreiben, und versucht – mit eiskalten Fingern und völlig durchgefroren – seine Aufnahmen zu machen.

Seit 400 Jahren kennt man in Mitteleuropa das Walroß aus abenteuerlichen Schilderungen und etwas verzerrten Zeichnungen. Erst seit wir die immer etwas distanziert und wahrheitsgetreu abbildenden Kameras haben gelingt es zu zeigen, wie perfekt die großen Körper funktionieren und wie die weichen Konturen der dunklen Tiere zu der sie umgebenden Landschaft aus Eis, Wasser und Schnee passen.

In the waters off the Jakeman glacier on Ellesmere Island chunks of floating icebergs in different sizes turn into resting places for the walrus even in the summer. To know this and to get there are two different things altogether. First you have to get to Winnipeg in Canada and from there on to Resolute Bay, the northern-most point connected by regular airline travel.

Once there you have to bide your time until a small Fokker will take you to the Eskimo settlements on Ellesmere Island. From there the journey continues by small boat with an outboard motor to the Jakeman glacier. After your arrival there you spend the night in the tents you brought yourself and spend the days in a boat searching the sea for floating icebergs until you are lucky enough to find one with resting walrus. You turn off the engine and let the water take you, at the same time carefully paddling closer, as you try to take your pictures – freezing and with ice-cold fingers.

For 400 years the walrus has been known in Central Europe through adventurous portrayals and somewhat distorted sketches. Only since we have cameras that we can take life-like pictures with from a distance have we been able to show clearly just how perfect the large bodies function and in what way the soft contours of the dark animals adjust to their surroundings of ice, water and snow.

Objectiv 2.8/24 mm, Kodachrome-64, Ellesmere Island, Canada

Schade...

What a Shame...

Womit haben sie das Bild gemacht? Wenn man dann antwortet: 'Mit einer XYZ und einem Zoom 80-200 mm', was sagt das und was beweist es?

Wenn man etwa im Ngorongoro Crater Elefanten im Morgennebel fotografieren will, dann muß man ein Zelt mitbringen und im Crater zelten, damit man zum Morgennebel dort ist. Wenn man in einer Lodge auf dem Craterrand übernachtet, dann ist der Morgennebel schon lange verflogen, wenn man unten ankommt. So einfach ist das.

Wenn man dann vor den Elefanten im Morgennebel steht, ist es völlig gleichgültig, ob man eine Canon EOS-3 benutzt, eine Nikon F-100 oder eine Minolta-, Leica- oder Pentax-SLR. Gute Fotos machen zu können setzt voraus, zur rechten Zeit am rechten Ort zu sein und – sein Handwerkszeug zu beherrschen.

Eine angesehene Kunstgalerie veranstaltete vor einigen Jahren eine Ausstellung mit 60 Bildern eines bekannten Naturfotografen. Als ein Kunde die Ausdrucksstärke der Fotografien lobte, antwortete die Galeristin freudestrahlend: 'Ja, nicht war, die hat er aber auch alle mit einer Minolta 9000 auf Kodachrome-25 gemacht'. Was ja wohl übersetzt heißt: Eigentlich ist dieser Naturfotograf ein Vollidiot, aber weil er eine Minolta 9000 hat und auf Kodachrome-25 fotografiert, gelingen ihm halt' gute Bilder'. – Intelektueller Höhenflug...

With what did you take that picture? If your answer is: with a xyz and a zoom of 80-200 mm, what does that say or prove?

If for instance you want to take pictures of elephants in the Ngorongoro Crater in the morning mist you have to bring a tent and camp out in the Crater over night in order to be there when the morning mist appears. If you stay in a lodge on the crater's edge you will get there too late to catch the mist. It is that easy.

Then, when you are standing in front of the elephants in the mist it is completely irrelevant if you are using a Canon EOS-3, a Nikon F-100 or a Minolta, Leica or Pentax -SLR. What makes the difference in taking good pictures is to be at the right place at the right time and – to know how to use your tools.

A renown art gallery hosted a show a few years ago with 60 pictures of a well-known nature photographer. When a customer praised the great expressiveness of these pictures, the gallery curator beamingly replied: "Yes, isn't that true....and he took all of the pictures with a Minolta 9000 on Kodachrome-25". Which if translated means: This nature photographer is a complete idiot but since he had a Minolta 9000 and was shooting on Kodachrome-25 he managed to take great pictures." – Intellectual nonsense...

Objectiv 4.0/80-200 mm, Kodachrome-64, Autoscheibenstativ – car tripod., Ngorongoro Crater, Tanzania

*Die Mutter Half Tail nimmt um 11.00 Uhr
Abschied von der toten Tochter.
Mother Half Tail parts with her dead
daughter at 11.00 am.*

**Es geht nicht darum, wie eine Wunschwelt
aussehen könnte – glatt, lieblich, durchgestylt,
sondern darum, wie die Wirklichkeit tatsächlich
ist. Durch die Arbeit der fotojournalistisch
arbeitenden Naturfotografen erfahren wir es.**
Kay Dohnke

**It is not about how a world you dream about
could look like – smooth, lovely and well-styled,
but about how reality actually is.
Through the photo journalistic work of nature
photographers we find out.**
Kay Dohnke

Leopards

Leoparden

Tragik und Glück liegen bekanntermaßen oft dicht bei-sammen. Seit Jahren hatte ich eine Leopardenfamilie in Kenias Wildreservat Masai Mara fotografiert: Die Mutter Half Tail und alle ihre Kinder. Die Leopardin hatte diesen Namen bekommen, weil sie bei einem Kampf mit Pavianmännchen den halben Schwanz verloren hatte.

Am Tage vor diesen beiden Aufnahmen hatte ich die Familie – Mutter und die 12 Monate alten Kinder Taratibu (die Vor-sichtige) und Manga'a (der Unbekümmerte) – noch bis Ein-bruch der Dunkelheit beobachtet.

Als ich am Morgen wieder da war, lag die Tochter tot auf dem Savannenboden – in der Nacht getötet von einer Löwin. Die Mutter saß 200 Meter von der toten Tochter ent-fernt auf einem kleinen Baum, und Sohn Manga'a – hatte eben die erste größere eigene Beute seines Lebens ge-macht – eine Thompsongazelle und auf einen hohen Baum gebracht und in der Krone versteckt .

Ich traf ihn dort am Morgen gegen 7.00 Uhr, und – er ver-ließ den Baum den ganzen Tag über nicht, und bewachte seine erste Beute. Den ganzen Tag über bot sich keine Ge-legenheit für ein interessantes Bild von ihm im Baum. Also hieß es warten, die Hauptbeschäftigung aller fotojourna-listisch arbeitenden Naturfotografen. Erst kurz vor Einbruch der Dunkelheit war die Situation reif für dieses Bild – nach fast elf Stunden.

Agony and ecstasy are known to lay close to one another. For years I had been photographing a leopard family in Kenya's wildlife reservation Masai Mara: the mother Half Tail and all her children. The female leopard got her name from having lost half her tail in a fight with a male baboon.

On the day before these pictures were taken I had observed the family – mother and the 12 month old offspring Tarat-ibu (the cautious) and Manga´a (the unburdened) – until darkness fell.

When I was there again in the morning, the daughter lay dead on the ground of the Savannah – killed during the night by a lioness. The mother sat 200 meters away from her dead daughter on a small tree, and son Manga´a – having just made the first kill of his life – a Thompson gazelle which he brought to the top of a high tree to hide.

I met him there in the morning about 7:00 AM, and he did not leave the tree all day, guarding his first kill. I did not have a good opportunity all day for an interesting picture of him in that tree. So that meant waiting, the main occupation of all working photo-journalistic nature photographers. Short-ly before sunset, at dusk, the situation was ready for me to take this picture – after almost eleven hours.

Objectiv 2.8/80-200 mm, Sensia-100, Autostativ – car tripod. Masai Mara, Kenya

Gnus – Wildebeest, Masai Mara, Kenya ▶▶

Manche Naturfotografen fühlen sich als Wissenschaftler, manche als Moralisten. Die Wissenschaftler mit der Kamera widmen sich der Bestandsaufnahme der Welt, die Moralisten konzentrieren sich auf schwierige Fälle.

Some nature photographers see themselves as scientists, some as moralists. The scientists with a camera dedicate themselves to the inventory of the world, the moralists concentrate on difficult cases.

Gefühle

Feelings

Die fotografisch ergiebigsten Momente in der Natur sind meistens diejenigen, in denen etwas passiert.

Löwen etwa, die einfach so schlafen, sind langweilig – und Löwen schlafen meistens. Man muß auf den entscheidenden Moment warten können, und man muß ihn kennen und wissen, wann er kommt.

Das junge Kätzchen um den Bart von Mama herumstreichen, ist ein altbekanntes Bild – alle Katzenarten tun es, und jeder, der zuhause Katzen hat, kennt den Vorgang ganz genau. Nur – ihn optimal zu fotografieren ist eine andere Geschichte. Man sieht es natürlich auch bei Löwen oft, dass die Kleinen von der Seite kommen und sich an Mutters Kopf vorbeischmiegen.

Aber: fast immer passiert dies in der Gruppe und am Boden zwischen allen anderen Löwen und mit viel Gestrüpp herum, es ist also weniger eine fotogene Situation als ein Beitrag zur Chaosforschung.

Schon seit Jahren wartete ich in der Masai Mara auf eine fotografisch günstige Situation, um dieses Motiv festzuhalten. Eines Tages kam ich angefahren und sah diese Löwin mit ihrem Kind auf einem Termitenhügel liegen – völlig frei, ohne andere Katzen drumherum, und als Bonus auch noch praktisch in Augenhöhe, also im optimalen Fotografierwinkel.

The most rewarding moments in nature are mostly those in which something happens.

Lions for instance that are just sleeping are boring – and lions sleep most of the time. You have to be able to wait for that decisive moment and you have to know it and see it coming.

The young feline swishing around mom's beard is a well-known picture – all types of cats do that and everyone who has cats at home knows the procedure exactly. Only – to take a picture of it is another story. Naturally you observe this with lions as well, that the young come from the side and rub against mother's head. But this happens almost always within the group and among brush and bushes which means a less photogenic situation and more of a contribution to the research of chaos.

For years I have been waiting in the Masai Mara for a picturesque situation in order to capture this motif. I drove up one day and saw this lioness with her cub lying on a termite hill – completely out in the open without any other feline around and as a bonus, practically at eye height – meaning a perfect photographic angle. The car had just stopped as the little one already swished past mother's head who obviously enjoyed this behavior and I had just a second for three takes with a motor drive…

Objectiv 4.0/600 mm, Velvia-50, Autoscheibenstativ – car tripod. Masai Mara, Kenya

Fledermausohrfüchse

Bat-eared Fox

**Wenn wir fotografieren leben wir,
der Rest ist nur warten.**

**When we take pictures we live,
the rest of the time is waiting**

Es gibt einen spannenden und einen langweiligen Weg, in Afrika zu fotografieren. Der spannende ist die Kamerajagd vom Auto aus. Man fährt am Morgen vor Sonnenaufgang hinaus und läßt sich überraschen, was wohl alles kommen wird: Vielleicht findet man Löwen, einen Leoparden mit Beute auf einem Baum, Elefanten, streitende Antilopen, eine Gepardin auf der Jagd oder Hyänen, die sich um Reste streiten.

Das macht Spaß und ist immer spannend, weil man nie weiß, was einen hinter dem nächsten Hügel erwartet.

Leider ist man bei dieser Art der Fotografie sehr vom Zufall abhängig. Besser ist der nicht so aufregende Weg, an einem Motiv dranzubleiben, es zu studieren und zu beobachten bis man entdeckt, wie man zu einem interessanten Bild kommen kann.

So war ich eine ganze Woche lang jeden Morgen – lange vor Sonnenaufgang – zu einem etwas entfernt liegenden Bau der Fledermausohrfüchse gefahren, um rechtzeitig zum ersten Fotolicht da zu sein.

Das interessanteste Foto, wenn alle kleinen Füchse zusammengeschmiegt aus dem Bau herausschauen, konnte man nämlich nur machen in der ersten halben Stunde des Tages, bevor die Sonne schien und es wärmer wurde. Denn wenn die Sonne schien, kuschelten sie nicht mehr und auch das Licht wurde viel zu hart.

There is an exciting and a boring way to take photographs in Africa. The exciting way is to go on a game drive by car. You drive out early in the morning, before dawn, and will be surprised about everything that happens: maybe you will find lions, a leopard with his kill in a tree, elephants, jousting antelopes, female cheetahs hunting or hyenas fighting over scraps.

It is fun and always exciting, because you never know what is waiting for you behind the next hill.

Sadly you are largely dependent on luck for this kind of photography. It is better to take the not-so-exciting way, to stay with a subject, to study and observe it, until you uncover how you can get an interesting picture.

It was like this for me the whole week, every morning – long before dawn – driving some way to the distant cave of the Bat-eared fox, to be there on time for the first photographic light.

The most interesting picture, when all the foxes were huddled together looking out of the cave, could only be made during the first half-hour of the day, before the sun shone and it got warmer. When the sun did shine they didn't huddle any more and the light turned too harsh.

Objectiv 4.0/600 mm, Fuji Sensia-100, Autoscheibenstativ – car tripod, Masai Mara, Kenya

Der Fotograf soll sich so wenig wie möglich einmischen, sonst geht jener objektive Charme verloren, den die Fotografie ihrer Natur nach besitzt.
Henri Matisse

The photographer should get involved as little as possible; otherwise the objective charm that is in the nature of photography is lost.
Henri Matisse

Symbiosis

Symbiose

Koexistenzen bei Tieren sind nicht selten. Wunderschön sichtbar sind sie in Ostafrika zwischen großen Säugern und den Gelbschnabel- und Rotschnabel-Madenhackern.

Sie benutzen Giraffen als Nahrungsquelle, Gazellen und Antilopen, Büffel, Weißbartgnus, halt' fast alles, was von Parasiten geplagt wird.

Eines der schönsten Bilder die ich hierbei je gesehen habe, aber leider nicht fotografieren konnte, war ein ganz kleines Warzenschwein, auf dessen Rücken wohl 14-16 Madenhacken saßen. Sie suchten dort wohl nicht nach Nahrung, sondern benutzten das Schwein als Landeplatz.

Blut trinkten sie auch: Ich traf einmal einen Löwen, der sich im Maul eines Büffels festgebissen hatte, und eine Viertelstunde lang nicht losließ. Dann konnte der Büffel sich losreißen. Er stand sichtbar unter Schock, und aus seinen Nasenlöchern floß das Blut. Nun kamen einige Madenhacker angeflogen, 'rutschen' von den Hörnern her kommend am Kopf des Büffels nach unten und tranken tropfenweise das Blut des Büffels.

Seltsamerweise sieht man nie Madenhacker auf Löwen, Geparden oder Leoparden, trotzdem da einiges zu holen ist. Manche Leoparden sind von Zecken förmlich übersäht, und ein Madenhacker wäre da eine Wohltat. Hier braucht die Evolution wohl noch einige Zeit, um diese Symbiose hinzukriegen.

Co-existence among animals is not a rarity. It is wonderfully visible in Eastern Africa between the great mammals and the red – or yellow – billed oxpecker.

They use giraffes, gazelles, antelopes, buffalo, burchell zebras – well, everything that is bothered with parasites, as a source of nourishment.

One of the nicest pictures I have seen but unfortunately couldn't take was a small warthog with about 14-16 oxpeckers on its back. I guess they were not looking for parasites there and just used it as a landing site.

They also drink blood: Once I met up with a lion that had locked its jaw while biting the mouth of a buffalo and would not let go for 15 min. Then the buffalo was able to tear loose. It was noticeably in shock and blood was flowing from its nostrils. Some oxpeckers came flying and slid down the horns from the top of the buffalo's head to drink the blood drop by drop.

Oddly enough, you never see oxpeckers on lions, cheetahs or leopards even though there would be a lot to get. Some leopards are practically covered with ticks and an oxpecker would be a blessing. In this case evolution will take some time to form that type of symbiosis.

Objectiv 3.5/400 mm & 2x Converter, Sensia-100, Scheibenstativ-car tripod, Masai Mara, Kenya

**Only when we understand can we care,
only when we care will we help,
only when we help shall they be saved.**
Jane Goodall

Relatives

Verwandtschaft

74

75

Die Abstammungslinien von Mensch und Schimpanse haben sich vor etwa fünf bis sieben Millionen Jahren getrennt. Zwischen Mensch und Gorilla ist es etwas länger her. Trotzdem haben wir noch eine genetische Ähnlichkeit von 98,7 % mit Schimpansen und Bonobos.

Wenn wir also alle zusammen nicht Menschen und Menschenaffen wären, sondern Käfer, dann würde man unsere Arten in eine gemeinsame Gattung stecken.

Die Wissenschaftler sind sich ja heute ziemlich einig, das unsere Art sich so vor 100.000 bis 200.000 Jahren in Ostafrika aus Frühmenschen heraus entwickelt hat.

Vor 40.000 Jahren sollen dann die ersten modernen Menschen in Europa eingewandert sein, und vor etwa 14.000 Jahren erreichten sie die Prärien Nordamerikas.

Wir haben zwar im Laufe dieser wenigen Jahrtausende einiges vom Affen in uns abgeschüttelt, aber manchmal möchte man doch Konrad Lorenz Recht geben, wenn er sagte: 'Das Bindeglied zwischen Affe und Mensch sind wir'. Denn wie wir mit unserer Verwandtschaft umgehen, spricht nicht für eine sehr weit entwickelte Intelligenz, Humanität und Verantwortung oder auch Mitgefühl bei uns.

So leben heute auf dem gesamten Planeten nur noch rund 650 Berggorillas, immerhin nach den Schimpansen unsere nächsten Verwandten. Keinen einzigen gibt es in Zoolo-

The line of descent from humans and chimpanzees separated about five to seven million years ago. It took a bit longer for the separation of gorrilas and humans.

In spite of that we still have a 98,7 genetic similarity with chimpanzees and bonobos.

So if we all were not human or primate but bugs, we would all be put into the same category.

Our scientists agree pretty much that our species evolved from the early humanoid 100.000 – 200.000 years ago in Eastern Africa.

40.000 years ago the first modern human is supposed to have immigrated to Europe and 14.000 years ago they reached the prairies of North America.

During the course of these few thousand years we shook off some of the primate behavior but at times we tend to agree with Konrad Lorenz when he said: "we are the connecting link between primates and humans."

Because the way we treat our relatives does not present evolved intelligence, humanity and responsibility or even sympathy in ourselves.

There are only about 650 mountain gorillas left alive on the entire planet today, after all, our closest relatives next to the chimpanzees.

There isn't a one in any zoo and if they can truly survive in

Objectiv 2.8/80-200 mm, Sensia-100 & Provia-400. Stativ – tripod.

Hand, Chimpanze
Gombe Stream National Park

Foot, Mountain Gorilla
Volcano National Park, Rwanda

Mountain Gorilla
Volcano Nationalpark, Rwanda

gischen Gärten. Und ob er im Virunga Massiv im Dreilän-
dereck Kongo, Uganda und Ruanda wirklich langfristig überleben kann, ist zweifelhaft.

Aber es ist leichter, 80 Milliarden Dollar für ein Kriegspro-
jekt zwischen Menschen in irgendeinem Parlament loszu-
eisen, als eine Million zum Schutz der letzten 650 noch über-
lebenden Verwandten, die einst sicher zu hunderttausenden
diesen Planeten bevölkerten.

Sie zu fotografieren ist etwas schwierig, weil wir natürlich
jedes Fleckchen Erde, mit dem wir glauben selber etwas an-
fangen zu können, für uns beanspruchen, Nur da, wo die
Berge so steil und unwirtlich werden, dass wir keine Felder
mehr anlegen können, gestatten wir großzügig einen kleinen Nationalpark für Gorillas.

the massive Virunga mountain range of the three corners
Congo, Uganda and Rwanda in the long run is doubtful.
On the other hand it is easier to pry loose 80 Billion Dollars
for a war project between people and some parliament then
one Million for the preservation of the remaining 650 relatives that at one time inhabited this planet by the hundreds
of thousands.

It is a bit difficult to catch them on film because every spot
of land on earth with which we believe we can do something with ourselves, has been claimed, naturally by us of
course. Only where the mountain sides are so steep that
we can't put fields on them do we generously allow a small
national park for gorillas.

Mountain Gorilla
Volcano National Park, Rwanda

Objectiv 2.8/80-200 mm & 2x Converter, Provia-400. Stativ – tripod.

Mahlzeit...

Chow-time...

Felsenphytons gehören in die Familie der Riesenschlangen, die gegen Ende der Kreidezeit entstanden ist.

Sie können Menschen durchaus gefährlich werden, und es sind Berichte verbürgt, dass sie welche angefallen und verschlungen haben.

Felsenphytons können recht große Tiere erbeuten und verspeisen. Dieser hier hatte im Nairobi Nationalpark in der Nacht eine ausgewachsene Impala-Antilope erbeutet und lag direkt neben ihr, als wir die beiden am Morgen in aller Frühe entdeckten. Wir blieben in respektvoller Entfernung stehen und warteten, was wohl passieren würde.

Nach etwa zwei Stunden fing die Schlange an, vom Kopf her das Beutetier zu fressen. Sie kann Ober- und Unterkiefer aus den Gelenken lösen – wie man auf diesen Fotos schön sehen kann – und dadurch die riesige Beute überhaupt erst verschlingen. Wenn sie ein so großes Beutetier verzehrt hat wie dieses hier, kann sie anschließend viele Wochen fasten. Unser Phython hier brauchte etwa fünf Stunden, bis er das Impala ganz verschlungen hatte und von der Beute nichts mehr zu sehen war.

Für den Naturfotografen ist so etwas ein Traummotiv: Er hat erstens alle Zeit der Welt und zweitens keinerlei technische Schwierigkeiten: Das Motiv ist Mittelton und leicht korrekt zu belichten, es läuft nicht davon, und man kann in aller Ruhe vom Stativ aus arbeiten.

Objectiv 4.0/80-200 mm, Kodachrome-64, Stativ – tripod.

African pythons are members of the family of giant snakes which evolved toward the end of the Cretaceous Period.

They certainly can be dangerous for humans, something that has been underlined through verified reports that humans have been attacked and devoured by them.

African pythons can capture and eat rather large animals. This one here had captured a grown impala antelope during the night in the Nairobi National Park and had it laying there beside it when we came across the two early in the morning.

We kept a respectful distance while watching and waiting what would happen.

After about two hours the snake started to devour the carcass starting with its head first. As you can see from these pictures very nicely, the snake has to unhinge its upper and lower jaws to even be able to swallow such gigantic spoils. After eating a large animal like this, the snake can fast for many weeks. Our python in the picture took about five hours before the antelope was swallowed completely and there was nothing of it left to see.

For the nature photographer this motif is like a dream come true: first of all he has all the time in the world and second, no technical problems to deal with. The subject has a mediocre tone and is easy to expose correctly, it doesn't run away and you can take the picture without rush off of a tripod.

Licht

**Das Glück hängt nicht davon ab,
was man weiß, sondern was man fühlt.**
Liberty Hyde Bailey

**Happiness does not depend on what
you know, but what you feel.**
Liberty Hyde Bailey

80
81

Das schönste Licht des Tages gibt es in Afrika vor Sonnenaufgang. Etwa eine halbe Stunde bevor der Sonnenball auftaucht, hat man für einige Minuten ein ganz wundervolles Licht.

Es ist nicht viel, aber von einer grandiosen Klarheit und Sauberkeit, von einer unglaublichen Intensität und Tiefe.

Es bringt die Landschaft und die Tiere zum Leuchten wie nie wieder am ganzen Tag. Weil es so schwach ist, muß man lange Belichtungszeiten nehmen oder einen hochempfindlichen Film.

Dieses Bild der aufmerksamen Impalagruppe machte ich in diesem Licht vor Sonnenaufgang deshalb mit einem 400-ISO-Film, den ich sonst nicht gerne nehme, weil die Farben wesentlich blasser kommen als bei einem 50- oder 100-ISO-Film. Das die Aufnahme trotzdem farblich so intensiv wurde, spricht für die einmalige Qualität dieses Lichtes vor Sonnenaufgang.

Man kann zu dieser Stunde am frühen Morgen vor Sonnenaufgang auch die schönsten Geparden-Porträts machen. Nie wieder am ganzen Tag haben diese Katzen die Augen so weit offen wie jetzt – nie wieder eine solche unergründliche Tiefe und Ausdruckskraft wie in diesen ganz frühen Minuten vor dem eben anbrechenden Tag. Die Seele der Natur offenbart sich vor Sonnenaufgang…

The best light of the day in Africa is before dawn. About half an hour before the ball of fire appears, you have really wonderful light for a few minutes.

It's not a lot, but with grand clarity and of such purity and unbelievable intensity and depth.

It makes the landscape and animals glow like at no other time during the day. Because it is so dim you have to use long shutter speeds or a highly sensitive film.

That is why I took this picture using 400-ISO-Film, which I normally don't prefer, because the colours appear paler then with a 50 or 100-ISO-Film, of a group of attentive Impala during this light before dawn. That this exposure came out as colorful as it did in spite of that, speaks for the quality of light before dawn. At this hour early in the morning before dawn you can also take the most beautiful portraits of cheetahs. At no other time during all the rest of the day do these cats have their eyes open so wide – such infinite depth and expression of power – as during the few minutes before the break of day. The soul of nature exposes itself before dawn…

Objectiv 4.0/600 mm, Fuji Provia-400, Autoscheibenstativ – car tripod. Masai Mara, Kenya

Crowned Head

Gekröntes Haupt

Zweieinhalb Stunden hatte ich bereits an einem Tümpel in der Nähe des Governor's Camp in Kenias Masai Mara gewartet. Fünfzehn bis zwanzig Flußpferde lagen dösend in ihm und tauchten nur manchmal auf. Schließlich war diesmal nicht dem Tüchtigen, sondern dem Geduldigen das Glück hold: Ganz in meiner Nähe präsentierte sich plötzlich ein wahrhaftes Prachtexemplar mit einer Naturkrone auf dem Kopf. Es sieht hier dick und gemütlich aus, aber wie gewöhnlich trügt der Schein. Flußpferde sind humorloser als die meisten großen Tiere, sie leben in engem Rudelverband in relativ kleinen Wasserrevieren und bevorzugen flaches Wasser. Sie sind ortstreu und mißtrauisch und mit ihren Eckzähnen sehr gefährlich, wenngleich Menschen selten gebissen werden.

Vor nicht einmal 100 Jahren machten sich sportliche Damen und Herren am unteren Nil einen Spaß daraus, vom Schiff aus auf die im Wasser ruhenden Tiere zu schießen. Nicht tödlich zwischen die Augen – das konnten sie vermutlich gar nicht. Einfach so...

Erfolg in der Naturfotografie beruht nicht auf der bestmöglichen Ausrüstung, sondern auf der Zeit, die man draußen verbringt. Je länger man ausharrt, je interessantere Bilder bekommt man. Bis ich ein Foto hatte wie oben: Kuhreiher auf Flußpferd, habe ich sicher weit über 300 Stunden bei Flußpferden gewartet.

I had already waited two and a half hours at a pond near the Governor's camp in Kenya's Masai Mara. Fifteen to twenty Hippos were laying in it dozing and only appearing on occasion. This time it was not the proficient but the patient who got lucky: very close to me, a truly perfect example presented itself with a natural crown on its head. It looks healthy and comfortable here but naturally looks can be deceiving. Hippopotamuses are more stoic than most big animals; they live in close-knit herds in relatively small waterholes and prefer shallow water. They are territorial and untrusting and can be dangerous with their teeth, albeit people have rarely ever been bitten.

Not even a 100 years ago, sporting ladies and gentlemen's idea of fun was going down the Nile taking shots at the peaceful water animals from their ship. Not mortally between the eyes – apparently they couldn't do that. Just because...

Success in nature photography does not depend on the best possible equipment, instead on the time spent outside. The longer you hold out, the more interesting pictures you get. Until I got the photo above, Cattle Egret on hippopotamus, I must have waited well over 300 hours with the hippos.

Objectiv 3.5/400 mm, 2x Converter, Sensia-100, Autoscheibenstativ, Car-tripod, Masai Mara, Kenya

Mutter

Mother

**Alle Technik der Welt kann die Unfähigkeit,
etwas zu bemerken, nicht kompensieren.**

Elliott Erwitt

**All the technology in the world can't compensate
for the inability to notice anything.**

Elliott Erwitt (adapted)

Viele Jahre folgte ich in Kenia einer Leopardenmutter mit meiner Kamera. Dabei konnte ich alle ihre Kinder fotografieren, die sie im Laufe der Jahre bekam. Mein Lieblingsbild unter den vielen die mir von dieser Familie gelangen, ist ohne Zweifel dieses Foto, wo die erste Tochter – die wir Beauty tauften – der Mutter ins Gesicht springt.

Was hier zwischen Mutter und Tochter vor sich geht, kann nur die Kamera erfassen, und nur die Naturfotografie kann uns solche vollkommenen Momente des Lebens schenken und sichtbar machen. Kein Blick und kein Gedanke kann dies erfassen. Nur die Kamera ist schnell genug.

Jeder der selber Katzen hat und sich mit ihrem Verhalten auskennt, wird dieses Bild mit großem Vergnügen betrachten. Denn die Tochter greift keineswegs die Mutter an. Sie attackiert zwar deutlich sichtbar mit offenem Maul, mit drohenden Reißzähnen und gewaltig gesträubten Schnurrhaaren, aber gleichzeitig hat sie die Ohren auf höchste Demutsstellung gedreht, und erklärt dadurch den Angriff zu einer Nullnummer.

Die Leopardenmama weiss dies natürlich, was man daran sehen kann, das sie die Ohren auf freundlich und den Schnurrbart auf behaglich gestellt hat. Und ihr Blick läßt sich deuten mit: Kind – geht es nicht etwas weniger wild? Die Aufnahme entstand 1993, und Beauty lebt heute (2004) noch in der Masai Mara.

For many years I followed a leopard mother with my camera in Kenya. During that time I was able to take pictures of all of the cubs she had throughout the years. My favorite picture among the many I was able to take from this family, is without a doubt this photo where her first female cub – we called her Beauty – jumps into her mother's face.

Only the camera can capture what happened here and only nature photography can present us with such perfect moments in life and in turn make them visible. There is not a glance or a thought that can capture this, only the camera is quick enough.

Everyone who has cats and is familiar with their behavior will look at this picture with great pleasure.

Because the daughter is in no way attacking her mother. She is assailing her with a clearly visible open mouth, with threatening fangs and greatly bristled whiskers but at the same time her ears are in a position of absolute devotion which turns this would-be attack into nothing.

The leopard mom is aware of this, which is plain to see by the way her ears are poised in a friendly position and her whiskers are signaling comfort.

The expression in her eyes gives us the impression of: kid – can you keep it down a little? This picture was taken in 1993, and Beauty is still alive today (2004) in the Masai Mara.

Objectiv 4.0/600 mm, Kodachrome-200, Autoscheibenstativ-car tripod. Masai Mara, Kenya

Bemalte Wölfe

Painted wolves

Solche Momente in der Natur kann nur die Fotografie festhalten. Zwei Wildhunde verfolgen 1988 in der Serengeti ein Gnu. Die Geschwindigkeit dieser Jagd kann man erahnen, wenn man genau hinschaut. Elf der zwölf Beine befinden sich in der Luft. Nur ein Wildhund berührt mit einem Fuß den Boden.

Wildhunde sind schneller und ausdauernder als Gnus. Daher ist ihre Jagdtechnik ganz einfach: Sie rennen neben dem Gnu her bis es nicht mehr kann und stehen bleibt. Dann hält es ein Wildhund an der Nase fest und die anderen reißen ihm den Magen auf. Das hat sie bei den Menschen sehr unbeliebt gemacht, weil es 'brutal' aussieht, und war mit ein Grund, warum sie stark bejagd wurden.

Auch haben sie große Probleme mit der Konkurrenz durch starke Hyänen-Clans und Löwenrudel, die ihnen die Beute streitig machen. In der Masai Mara und der Serengeti sind sie leider so gut wie verschwunden, wobei alle Erklärungen nicht so ganz zu überzeugen vermögen. Das letzte große Rudel von 20-30 Wildhunden hatte 1988 in der Masai Mara einen Bau mit Jungen im Gebiet der Aitong-Berge. Sie haben Millionen Jahre überlebt, warum verschwinden sie gerade jetzt, wo sie völlig unter Schutz gestellt sind?

Selbst die intensiven Schutzimpfungen zwischen 1980 und 1990 haben es nicht vermocht, ihre Existenz in Ostafrika zu sichern.

Moments like these in nature can only be captured by photography. Two wild dogs were chasing a gnu in the Serengeti 1988. If you look closely, you can imagine the speed of this chase. Eleven of the twelve legs are up in the air. Only one of the wild dogs has a foot touching the ground.

Wild dogs are faster and more persistent then gnus. Their hunting technique is really quite simple: they run alongside the gnu until it is exhausted and stops. Then one of the wild dogs holds on to the nose of one and the others will tear the belly open. That is why they became unpopular with people, since it appears to be brutal and was one of the reasons why they were frequently hunted.

They also have great problems with competitors like strong clans of hyenas and lions who challenge them with their prey. Unfortunately they have all but disappeared in the Masai Mara and the Serengeti and some of the explanations are not quite convincing. The last large band of wild dogs consisting of 20-30 dogs had a burrow with pups in 1988 in the area of the Aitong Mountains. They survived millions of years so why are they disappearing now, just when they have been taken into preservation? Not even the intense inoculations between 1980 and 1990 were able to secure their existence in East Africa.

Objectiv 4.0/300 mm, Kodachrome-200, Serengeti National Park, Tanzania

Wir alle bewegen uns am Rande der Ewigkeit.
Und manchmal wird uns ein Blick
durch den Stoff der Illusion gewährt.
Ansel Adams

We all are moving on the edge of eternity and
sometimes we are allowed to take a glimpse
through the material of illusion.
Ansel Adams

Ringelreigen

Ring Around The Rosies

Das Leben ist nicht fair, auch nicht in der so oft beschworenen 'herrlichen und wundervollen Natur'. Gepardinnen etwa jagen am liebsten trächtige Weibchen (wie oben links im Bild), weil die naturgemäß während der Schwangerschaft nicht so schnell sind und daher leichter zu erbeuten. Denn Nahrung zu erjagen ist ein schwieriges und gefährliches Geschäft und das macht man sich natürlich nicht unnötig schwer. Am Staub hinter der Gepardin und an der Stellung des Schwanzes, mit dem sie den abrupten Richtungswechsel ausbalanciert, kann man das Tempo dieser Verfolgungsjagd erahnen.

Geparde müssen lernen zu jagen und vor allem Beute zu schlagen und sie zu ersticken, sonst können sie nicht überleben. Was auf dem großen Bild wie ein Ringelreigen-Spiel mit einem kleinen Impala aussieht, ist in Wirklichkeit hartes Training für das kommende Leben der kleinen Geparde alleine in der Savanne, wenn die Mahlzeiten nicht mehr von Mama serviert werden.

Hier übten die vier kleinen Geparde etwa zwei Stunden mit dem Impala, bevor Mutter Gepardin es tötete und alle fünf es gemeinsam verzehrten. So oder so ist das Leben…

Life is not fair, not even in the so often called "wonderful and glorious nature". Female cheetahs for instance like hunting pregnant females (as seen in the picture to your upper left), since they are naturally not as fast and as such easier to catch. It is a difficult and dangerous task to hunt for nourishment, so naturally you don't make it any more difficult then it already is. You can guess the speed of the chase by the dust behind the cheetah and the way she holds her tail with which she balances herself out during abrupt changes of direction.

Cheetahs have to learn how to hunt and most of all how to slay their prey by choking them or they will not survive themselves. What looks like a "Ring around the rosies" game with the little impala is in reality hard training for the upcoming life of the little cheetahs in the savannah, when the meals will not be served by mom any longer.

Here the four cheetah cubs were practicing with the impala for two hours before mother cheetah killed it and the five of them ate it together.

This or that… either way, such is life.

Objectiv 4.0/300 mm, Sensia-100, Scheibenstativ – car tripod. Masai Mara, Kenya

Für ein gutes Foto braucht man 20 Jahre und 1/125 Sekunde.

For a good picture you need 20 years and 1/125 seconds.

Tripod

Stativ

Stativ hatten wir dieses Krokodil im Mara River getauft, weil ihm irgendwie ein Hinterbein abhanden gekommen war, und es deshalb mit drei Beinen durch das Leben kommen mußte, was aber für ein Krokodil nicht so problematisch ist wie für andere Tiere.

Auf jeden Fall schien es keine Nachteile durch dieses fehlende Bein zu haben. Es hatte sich ein besonders günstiges Stück im Marafluß erobert, wo immer in der Wanderzeit tausende von Weißbartgnus den Fluß durchquerten und wo es also reichlich und sicher gute Beute gab.

Allerdings sind Krokodile nicht besonders scharf auf Gnufleisch: Sie erbeuten zwar die Gnus und fressen sie auch, aber Zebras oder Gazellen sind ihnen wesentlich lieber. Wenn eine Gnuherde den Fluß durchquert, lassen sie diese oft unbehelligt ziehen, wenn sie die Chance sehen, an Zebra- oder Gazellenfleisch zu kommen.

Die gleiche Beobachtung habe ich auch oft bei Löwenrudeln gemacht. Die erbeuten oft Kaffernbüffel und lassen sie dann tot, aber unangetastet liegen, wenn sie plötzlich die Chance sehen, ein Zebra zu erbeuten. Anscheinend schmeckt beiden Arten Zebrafleisch wesentlich besser.

Hier auf den beiden Bildern hat 'Stativ' eine Grantgazelle erbeutet. Wie es die Beute hält zeigt an, dass das Krokodil sie auf die Wasseroberfläche aufklatschen will. Das machen Krokodile, um Fleischbrocken zu lösen.

We had named this crocodile in the Mara River "Tripod" because it seemed to have lost one of its legs somewhere along the line and had to go through life with only three legs, which is not quite as bad for a crocodile then another animal.

In any case it did not seem to be having any disadvantages through the missing leg. It had managed to claim an especially favorable spot in the Mara River where thousands of travelling gnus crossed the river during the migration period of wildebeest which certainly provided for more then enough prey.

On the other hand, crocodiles are not especially fond of gnu-meat – they will grab and eat them, but they like zebras or gazelles much better. They will let a herd of gnus cross the river without touching them if they have a chance to get zebra or gazelle meat. I have often made the same type of observation with packs of lions. They frequently slay African buffalos but leave the carcass untouched if they happen to see a chance to take a zebra. It seems that both types of animals prefer the taste of zebra to other meat.

On these two pictures here you see that Tripod had slain a Grant gazelle. It is obvious that the crocodile wants to slam its pray onto the surface of the water by the way it is holding it. Crocodiles are known to do this in order to loosen chunks of meat.

Objectiv 4.0/600 mm, Ektachrome-100, Autoscheibenstativ – car tripod, Masai Mara, Kenya

**Wer noch staunen kann,
wird auf Schritt und Tritt beschenkt.**
Oskar Kokoschka

**Those who can yet be amazed
will be awarded every step along the way.**
Oskar Kokoschka

Happy

Glücklich

Leopardenfotografie macht depressiv. Man wartet den ganzen Tag zwischen Büschen, Bäumen und Gräben, das er sich bewegt. Aber er bleibt versteckt, weil er genau weiß, das alle Tiere warnen, sobald er sich sehen läßt. Erst in der – fotografisch gesehen – letzten Minute vor der Dunkelheit wird er aktiv. Aber dann ist es oft zu spät für gute Fotos. Gepardenfotografie dagegen macht heiter. Geparde sind den ganzen Tag über in der offenen Savanne und liegen gerne weithin sichtbar auf Termitenhügeln. Wenn sie jagen, dann für den Naturfotografen gut sichtbar in freundlichem Gelände. Es macht Spaß, Geparde aufzunehmen.

Sie sind die schnellsten Säugetiere der Welt, mit rund 120 km in der Stunde auf kurzer Strecke. Allerdings ist so ein 'fliegender' Gepard nicht so leicht zu bekommen, weil er meistens erst gemächlich losgeht, und erst auf den letzten Metern diese schwebende Position einnimmt. Sechs Wochen Gepardenfotografie – ohne andere Motive – von 6.00 Uhr am Morgen bis 6.00 Uhr am Abend waren nötig, um dieses Bild zu bekommen.

Eines Morgens wartete ich bei einer Gepardin mit einem kleinen Jungen, als plötzlich ein Insektenschwarm auftauchte, und für wenige Augenblicke über ihnen kreiste. Der kleine Gepard schaut ganz erstaunt zu diesem, vielleicht ersten Insektenschwarm seinens Lebens. Ein kurzer, zauberhafter Moment.

Leopard photography is depressing. You wait all day among bushes, trees and ditches for him to move. But he stays hidden. He knows perfectly well that as soon as he is discovered, all the animals will send up an alarm. Only during – from a photographer's view – the last minute of light before darkness will he be active, but then most of the time it is too late for good pictures.

Photographing cheetahs on the other hand is motivating. Cheetahs are in the open savannah throughout the whole day and like to lie on termite hills to be seen far and wide. When they hunt, then quite visible for the nature photographer, in friendly terrain. It is fun to capture cheetahs.

They are the fastest mammals in the world at about 120kph on short stretches. It is not easy to get one of those "flying" cheetahs since he starts out slow and not until the last few meters does he have that floating position. Six weeks of cheetah photography – no other subjects – from 6am to 6pm were necessary in order to get this picture.

One morning I was waiting with a female cheetah and her cub when suddenly a swarm of insects appeared and circled above them for a few moments. The tiny cheetah, surprised, peered at maybe the first insect swarm of his life. A short but enchanting moment.

Objectiv 4.0/300 mm, Sensia-100, Scheibenstativ – car tripod, Masai Mara, Kenya

Ich liebe den Schnee.
Er lehrt uns Respekt vor der Natur.
Hartmut Grassl

I love the snow.
Snow teaches us respect for nature.
Hartmut Grassl

Die Entdecker

Die Schneeaffen sind als Erfinder und Entdecker bekannt. Sie waschen Getreidekörner im Wasser, baden in heißen Quellen und spielen in ihren jungen Jahren mit Steinen und Schneebällen.

Die Affenfamilien kommen in regelmäßigen Abständen zu den heißen Quellbecken und baden dann darin völlig ungestört. Es ist erstaunlich, daß sie sich nicht erkälten, wenn sie mit klatschnassem Fell im Wald verschwinden. Auch die Biologen in Japan wissen bis heute nicht, warum sich die Schneeaffen keinen Schnupfen holen. Vielleicht hilft das dichte Unterfell.

Kartoffel und Getreide im Meer zu waschen und Schneebälle zu formen um damit zu spielen, das hat diese Rotgesichtsmakaken weltberühmt gemacht. Allerdings habe ich im Joshin-Etsu kogen Nationalpark in den japanischen Alpen in der Nähe von Nagano immer nur gesehen, daß junge Tiere Schneebälle formen um damit zu spielen, obwohl dies für ältere, erfahrene Tiere sicher noch einfacher wäre. Anscheinend ist der Spieltrieb bei jungen Tieren viel ausgeprägter als bei älteren, wie beim Menschen und wie ja auch bei den Galapagos-Bussarden zu sehen ist.

An und für sich bin ich ein Stativ-Fetischist, aber hier bei den Schneeaffen habe ich zum ersten Mal in meinem Fotografenleben lieber mit dem Einbeinstativ gearbeitet.

Japanese macaques or snow monkeys are well known as explorers and inventors. They wash grain in water, bathe in hot springs and when they are young they play with rocks and snowballs.

The families come to the hot springs on a regular basis and take their baths there unencumbered. It is amazing that they do not catch colds when they disappear in the woods with their soaking wet fur. Even the Japanese biologists have no idea why these monkeys do not catch colds. Maybe the dense undercoat of their fur helps.

What has made these red-faced macaques famous throughout the world is that they wash potatoes and grain in water and they form snowballs for the purpose of fun and games. In the Joshin-Etsu kogen National Park I only observed the younger animals forming snowballs and playing with them, although it would have been easier to do for the older ones. It seems that the playfulness is not as predominant in the older animals as it is in the younger ones; this is similarly observed in us humans and the buzzard-like Galapagos hawk.

Under normal circumstances I am more of a tripod fetishist but here with these snow monkeys I used a one-legged camera stand. Nowadays with the availability of lenses that have stabilizers I might even take these pictures free handed.

Objectiv 2.8/80-200 mm, Sensia-100, Joshin-Etsu kogen National Park, Japan

**Geduld ist die Kraft,
mit der wir das Beste erlangen.**
Konfuzius

**Patience is the power
with which we can achieve the best.**
Confucius

*Drei Spuren von Schneeleoparden:
zwei bergauf und eine bergab.
Three tracks of snow leopards:
Two uphill and one downhill*

Snow Leopards

Schneeleoparden

Sehnsucht nach menschlicher Nähe ist sicher nicht das Problem von Schneeleoparden. Georg Schaller war der erste dem es gelang, 1970 einen freilebenden in der Hindu Kush Region des Himalaya in Pakistan zu fotografieren. Nur wenige weiße Menschen haben ihn überhaupt je in Freiheit gesehen.

Nachdem ich mich intensiv mit afrikanischen Leoparden beschäftigt hatte, hielt ich es für eine gute Idee, dem Oeuvre der Naturfotografie einige Bilder dieser geheimnisvollen Katze Asiens hinzuzufügen, und reiste dafür im Juli 1995 ins Altai-Gebirge der Mongolei.

Da stand ich nun zu Fuß mit meiner Kamera in einigen tausend Meter Höhe im völlig kahlen und baumlosen Gebirge und konnte kilometerweit sehen – eventuell vorhandene Schneeleoparden allerdings auch.

Keine Spuren waren zu sehen und ich sagte zu mir: Pölking, du bist der größte Trottel unter allen lebenden oder jemals gelebt habenden Naturfotografen und – reiste wieder ab. Meinen zweiten Versuch startete ich dann im Januar 1996 – mit Schnee und zu Pferde im Gobi Nationalpark.

Jetzt konnte ich die Höhenrücken der Berge abreiten und nach Spuren suchen. Nach drei Wochen begegnete ich zwei Schneeleoparden – Geschwister –, die wenig Scheu vor mir zeigten. Wahrscheinlich war ich der erste Mensch, dem sie je begegnet waren.

The desire for closer human contact is certainly not the problem of snow leopards. George Schaller was the first to succeed, in the Hindu Kush region of the Himalayas in Pakistan to take photographs in 1970. Only a few white people have ever seen one in the wilderness.

Only after I had intensively studied African leopards, did I consider it a good idea to provide nature-photography with several pictures of these secretive cats in Asia, and travelled to the Altai-Mountains of Mongolia in July, 1995.

There I stood, on foot, with my camera, at several thousand meters altitude in a totally barren and treeless mountain range and could see for miles – as well as possible existing snow leopards.

No tracks could be seen and I said to myself: Pölking, you are the biggest fool among all nature photographers living or dead – and departed.

Then, I started my second attempt in January 1996 – this time with snow as well as horses, in the Gobi National Park. This time I could work the high mountain range and look for tracks. After three weeks I was met by two snow leopards – siblings – who showed little fear of me. I was probably the first person they had ever come across.

Objectiv 4.0/80-200 mm, Sensia-100, Stativ/ tripod, Altai Mountains, Mongolia

Olmsted Point – Jeffrey pine, granite bolder & raven

Heaven

Himmel

Wenn es ein Paradies auf Erden für Landschaftsfotografen gibt, dann ist dies der Yosemite Nationalpark in Kalifornien. Hier machte im letzten Jahrhundert auch Ansel Adams seine berühmten schwarzweißen Landschaftsbilder.

If there is a paradise on earth for landscape photographers, then it would have to be Yosemite National Park in California. This is where Ansel Adams took his famous black and white landscapes during the last century.

▲ *Objectiv 4.0/70-200 mm, Fujichrome Velvia-50, Stativ - tripod.*
▶ *Objectiv 4.0/17-40 mm, Fujichrome Velvia-50, Stativ - tripod.*

Merced River & El Capitan at sunset

Glacier Point mit Half Dom im Kreislauf des Tages.
Glacier Point with the Half Dome all during the course of a day.

Objectiv 4.0/17-40 mm, Fujichrome Velvia-50,
Polarisations-Filter, Stativ - tripod.

Zitterpappelblätter – vom Winde bewegt
Aspen leaves – moved by the breeze

Yosemite national park

Objectiv 4.0/70-200 mm & 2x converter,
Fujichrome Velvia-50, Stativ - tripod. ▲

Objectiv 4.0/17-40 mm, Fujichrome Velvia-50,
Pol-Filter, Stativ - tripod. ▶▶

Naturfotografie ist ein Weg zu erzählen
was man fühlt über das, was man sieht.
Ansel Adams

Nature photography is a way to
say what you feel about what you see.
Ansel Adams

The moment between life and death
Der Moment zwischen Leben und Tod

Wenn sich ein Fischadler aus zehn Meter Höhe herabstürzt, um stoßtauchend bis zu einem Meter unter der Wasser-oberfläche einen lebenden Fisch zu erbeuten, dann ist dies ein wirklich dramatischer Moment in der Natur, der uns tief unter der Oberfläche der Schönheit dem Tod bei der Arbeit zusehen läßt.

Leben und Tod sind hier untrennbar miteinander verbunden: Ist der Adler erfolgreich, stirbt der Fisch. Lernt es ein Adler nicht, unter Wasser Fische zu erbeuten, stirbt der Adler.
Nur die Naturfotografie kann die Ambivalenz solcher Augenblicke festhalten. Nur sie kann diesen magischen Moment für immer sichtbar machen. Alle anderen Künste werden in solchen Situationen zu Fußnoten.
Die moderne fotografische Art der Wahrnehmung, entstanden durch den Einfluß der Fotografie auf den menschlichen Blick, verwirklicht sich hier in der Gleichzeitigkeit von Traum und Realität, und das Rauschhafte der Assoziation wird festgehalten durch die Möglichkeiten der modernen Naturfotografie mit Autofokus und Motordrive, und dadurch wird die fast unsichtbare Dauer des Augenblicks als Erlebnis für immer eingefroren.
Wahrscheinlich deshalb hat schon Konfuzius gesagt: 'Verglichen mit der Naturfotografie ist alles andere Unsinn'.

When an osprey plummets down 10 meters to dive almost one meter below the surface of the water in order to catch a live fish, then it is this that really dramatizes that moment in nature which lets us see down deep under the surface of beauty to watch death at work.
Life and death are inseparably connected with each other: is the osprey successful, the fish dies; does the osprey not learn to catch fish below the water's surface, the osprey dies.
Only the nature photographer can capture the mixed emotions of such moments. Only this can make this magical moment visible forever. All other forms of art become footnotes in such situations.
The modern type of this photographic way of perception, derived from the influence of photography through human eyes, becomes real here in the simultaneousness of dream and reality and the euphoria from this association is captured through the possibilities of modern nature photography with auto focus and motor drive, and through this the almost invisible duration of the moment is frozen forever as experience.
That is probably the reason why Confucius said: everything else is nonsense in comparison to nature photography.

Objectiv 4.0/500 mm, Fujichrome Sensia-400, Stativ – tripod. Kangasala, Finland.

Fischadler
Osprey

Objectiv 2.8/300 mm,
Fujichrome Sensia-100

Lake Asnen,
Sweden

Fischadler
Osprey

Objectiv 4.0/500 mm,
Fujichrome Sensia-400

Kangasala,
Finland.

Fischadler
Osprey

Objectiv 4.0/500 mm,
Fujichrome Sensia-400

Kangasala,
Finland.

Fischadler
Osprey

Objectiv 4.0/500 mm,
Fujichrome Sensia-400

Kangasala,
Finland.

Fragen & Antworten

Hatten Sie Vorbilder?
Aber ja: Hermann Fischer-Warenholz und Eric Hosking.

Welches berühmte Foto hätten Sie gerne auf-genommen?
Die Pinguine auf einem blauen Eisberg von Cherry Alexander.

Welche Gabe fehlt ihnen?
Geduld – mit Ausnahme wenn ich vor einem Motiv warte, dann habe ich sie.

Ihr Erfolgsgeheimnis?
Es gibt vier: Unbeirrt dranbleiben und Selbstkritik, Selbst-kritik, Selbstkritik.

Kollegen?
Manchmal wird man mit Neid und Mißgunst konfrontiert. Aber das passiert wohl jedem, der Erfolg hat.
Ich persönlich arbeite gerne mit anderen Naturfotografen zusammen. Ich habe schon drei Bücher mit Kollegen zu-sammen gemacht, und in unserer Naturfotografengruppe 'Blende4.com' arbeiten wir mit viel Vergnügen zusammen an Projekten, und fotografieren oft gemeinsam die gleichen Motive.

Welche fotografischen Leistungen bewundern Sie am meisten:
Die Wildlife-Fotos von Jonathan Scott, die Nahaufnahmen von John Shaw, die Landschaften von Art Wolfe und die Fotostory's von Frans Lanting.

Was bringt die Zukunft?
Die Naturfotografen werden meiner Ansicht nach versu-chen, mehr Geschichten in ihren Bildern zu erzählen.

Fotografieren Sie zur Zeit analog oder digital?
Meine Arbeitsfotos, Spaßfotos und die Kontrollbilder – für die man früher Polaroid nahm – fotografiere ich digital mit der EOS-300 D.
Die 'ernsthaften' Bilder mache ich auf Diafilm.

Warum?
Ich bin mir noch nicht sicher, ob und wann ich umsteigen soll. Sport- und Pressefotografen wurden praktisch gezwun-gen schnell umzusteigen. Naturfotografen können ganz gelassen abwarten.

Man soll also warten?
Nicht unbedingt. Wem die digitale Fotografie Spaß macht und wer gerne am Computer sitzt, sollte direkt umsteigen. Vorsichtig abwarten gilt mehr für Profis und Semisprofis.

Wieso?
Viele Agenturen erwarten als Qualitätsminimum für Bilder die redaktionell veröffentlicht werden sollen Datensätze mit 6 Millionen Pixel, und für Aufnahmen für die Werbung 11 Millionen Pixel.
Ein Sensia-100 Film liefert aber im Kleinbildformat schon 25 Millionen Pixel und ein Velvia-100 satte 50 Millionen Pixel. Es gibt also keinen Grund zur Eile.
Je länger man wartet, je besser, billiger und einfacher in der Bedienung wird praktisch alles, was man zur digitalen Fo-tografie benötigt.
Im Augenblick (2004) arbeite ich analog mit der EOS-1 V und scanne die Dias mit einem Nikon Coolscan 4000 ED für mei-ne Agenturen und sende denen CD-Rom's, und für die Kun-den welche weiterhin Dias bevorzugen oder große Kalen-der drucken wollen, habe ich die Originaldias.

Questions & Answers

Did you have any role models?
Absolutely: Hermann Fisher-Warenholz and Eric Hosking.

Which famous picture would you have liked to have taken?
The penguins on a blue colored ice berg by Cherry Alexander.

Which talent are you lacking?
Patience – unless I am waiting in front of my subject, that is when I do have it.

What is the secret to your success?
There are four: unwavering diligence and self-criticism, self-criticism, self-criticism.

Colleagues?
Sometimes you are confronted with envy and malevolence, but I think that happens to everyone who is successful.
I personally like to work together with other nature photographers. I have already done 3 books with colleagues and in our club of nature photographers "blende4.com" we work on projects together with pleasure and often take pictures of the same subject at the same time.

Which great photographic feats do you admire the most?
The wildlife pictures of Jonathan Scott, the close-ups from John Shaw, the landscapes by Art Wolfe and the photo stories from Frans Lanting.

What will the future bring?
The nature photographers will try to tell more stories with their pictures. In my opinion.

Are you currently taking analog or digital pictures?
Pictures I work with, fun-photos and the pictures I use for check-up – the ones that I used to with a Polaroid – I do digitally with the EOS-300 D. The more serious pictures are taken as slides.

Why?
I am not sure yet if and when I should switch. Sports and press photographers were practically forced to change quickly. Nature photographers can stay cool and take their time.

So one should wait?
Not necessarily. If you are having fun with digital photography and sitting at the computer, you should switch directly. Waiting cautiously is meant more for pros and semi-pros.

How come?
The majority of the agencies expect data files with 6 million pixels as minimum quality for pictures they would use editorial and for advertisements it is 11 million pixels.
A Sensia – 100 film will give you 25 million pixels alone in the 35 mm format and a Velvia – 100 all of 50 Million. So there is no reason to hurry.
The longer you wait, the better, less expensive and easier to use they will get, like everything else you will need for digital photography.
At the moment (2004) I am working analog with the EOS-I V and am scanning the slides with the Nikon Coolscan 4000 ED for my agencies, sending them CD ROMs; as for the customers that continue to prefer slides or want to print large calendars, I have and use the originals.

Ausrüstung • Equipment

1955 - 1965:	Leica IIIf & Telyt 4.5/200 mm
1965 - 1975:	Edixa & Noflexar 5.6/400 mm
1975 - 1985:	Olympus OM-2 & Zuiko Lenses
1985 - 2000:	Nikon F3, F4, F5 & Nikon Lenses
2000 - ? :	Canon EOS-1 V & Canon Lenses

Film
Fujichrome Sensia-100 (Wildlife)
Fujichrome Velvia-50 (Landscape)

Kameras • Cameras
Analog: Canon EOS-1 V
Digital: Canon EOS 300 D

Objektive • Lenses
Meistbenutzte: Most used:
17-40 mm/4.0
28-105 mm/3.5-4.5
70-200 mm/4.0
500 mm/4.0

Selten benutzte: Seldom used:
180 mm/3.5
70-200 mm/2.8
400 mm/4.0

Zubehör • Accessories
Converter 1.4x & 2x

Filter:
81-A Warming filter
Circular polarizer
1- and 2- stop graduated

neutral density filter

Kabelauslöser
Remote release cabel

Zwischenringe -
Extension tubes:
12 mm & 25 mm

Nahlinse:
Closeup lens:
Canon 500 D

Blitz/Flash:
Canon Speedlite 550 EX

Lichtmesser:
Incident light meter:
Gossen Variosix F2

Photoflex Aufheller gold/silber
Photoflex Diffuser

Photoflex Litedisc gold/silver
diffuser and reflector

Stativ/Tripod:
Gitzo Carbon 1227

Kugelkopf/Ballhead:
Kirk B-1

Internet: www.poelking.com

Bücher von Fritz Pölking

DEUTSCH

Am Puls des Lebens
2004, Kilda Verlag
ISBN 3-88949-201-0.

Werkstattbuch Naturfotografie
2003, Hoyer Verlag,
ISBN 3-929192-17-9.

Die große Fotoschule Natur
2003, Knaur Verlag,
ISBN 3-426-66733-9.

Momente der Natur
2002, Tecklenborg Verlag
ISBN 3-934427-18-9.

Die Tierwelt im Sucher
2000 Augustus Verlag,
ISBN 3-8043-5141-7.

Fritz Pölking's Image Collection
1999, Kilda Verlag,
ISBN 3-88949-196-0.

Tierfotografie
1998, Augustus Verlag,
ISBN 3-8043-5116-6.

Nahfotografie in der Natur
1997, Augustus Verlag,
ISBN 3-8043-5097-6.

Störche (mit Uwe Walz)
1996, Tecklenborg Verlag,
ISBN 3-924044-25-2.

Masai Mara
1995, Tecklenborg Verlag
ISBN 3-924044-16-3.

Naturfotografie
1995, Augustus Verlag,
ISBN 3-8043-5038-0.

Leoparden
1995, Tecklenborg Verlag,
ISBN 3-924044-17-1.

Der Leopard (mit W. & H. Hagen)
1995, Tecklenborg Verlag
ISBN 3-924044-21-X.

Fotoprojekt Masai Mara
1995, Gesellschaft Deutscher
Tierfotografen e.V.

Geparde (mit Norbert Rosing)
1993, Tecklenborg Verlag,
ISBN 3-924044-11-2.

Vogelfotografie
1977, Kilda Verlag,
ISBN 3-88949-112-X.

Nationalpark Galapagos
1977, Kilda Verlag,
ISBN 3-88949-160-X.

Wie fotografiert man Vögel?
1971, Franckh-Kosmos Verlag,
ISBN 3-440-03773-8.

Weiterführende
Informationen zu diesen
Büchern finden Sie unter:
www.poelking.com

Books by Fritz Pölking

ENGLISH

At the Pulse of Life
2004, Kilda Verlag,
ISBN 3-88949-201-0

The Art of Wildlife Photography
1998, Fountain Press,
ISBN 0-86343-322-7.

Fritz Pölking's Image Collection
1999, Kilda Verlag,
ISBN3-88949-196-0.

FRENCH

Planete sauvage
2001, Editions Proxima,
ISBN 2-84550-084-X.

CHINESE

自然摄影
2003, Liaoning Science and
Technology Publishing House,
ISBN 7-5381-3761-0.

DUTCH

Hoe fotografeert men vogels?
1972, W. J. Thieme Verlag
ISBN 90-03-94600-0

You can find follow-up
information to these books
under:
www.poelking.com

Fritz Pölking
Junger Berggorilla
Virunga Vulkane, Ruanda

Fritz Pölking   *Eisbär im Sommer*   Hudson Bay, Kanada

Wenn Ihnen eine Aufnahme in diesem Buch
besonders gut gefällt, dann können Sie dieses
Bild als Poster oder Kunstdruck bestellen bei:

If there is a picture that appeals to you in
a special way you have the possibility
to order it as a poster or an art print from:

celebration of nature

Petra Pölking – Riehler Str. 31 – 50668 Köln – Germany
Phone +49 (0) 221 – 1 20 77 50 Fax +49 (0) 221 – 1 20 77 51
www.celebration-of-nature.com
info@celebration-of-nature.com

Leopardin mit Jungem in der Dämmerung ▶▶
Leopardess & cub in twilight.
Masai Mara, Kenya